Cress Delahanty

BY JESSAMYN WEST

DRAWINGS BY JOE KRUSH

HARCOURT, BRACE AND COMPANY

NEW YORK

TO CARMEN

Some sections from this book appeared originally, in a somewhat different form, in the following magazines: *The New Yorker, The Ladies' Home Journal, Harper's Magazine, Collier's, Woman's Day, The New Mexico Quarterly,* and *The Colorado Quarterly.*

CONTENTS

PART I

Twelve

Fall

"I, Cress," said the girl, "in the October day, in the dying October day." She walked over to the fireplace and stood so that the slanting sunlight fell onto her bare shoulders with a red wine stain. The ashes smelled raw, rain wet. Or perhaps it's the water on the chrysanthemums, she thought, or the bitter, autumn-flavored chrysanthemums themselves.

She listened for her second heart-beat, the tap of the loosened shingle. But it was dead, it beat no more. For three days the Santa Ana had buffeted the house, but now at evening it had died down, had blown itself out. It was blown out, but it left its signs: the piled sand by the east doorsills; the tumbleweeds caught in the angle of the corral; the signboard by the electric tracks, face down; the eucalyptus with torn limb dangling.

"The Sabbath evening," said the girl, "the autumn Sabbath evening." And glowing and warm against the day's sober death, the year's sad end, burned her own bright living.

She walked to her own room, across her fallen night-gown, past her unmade bed, and opened the casement

13

window and leaned out toward the west. There the sun was near to setting, red in the dust, and the lights in the distant well-riggings already blazed. She watched the sun drop until the black tracery of a derrick crossed its face.

"The day dies," murmured the girl, "its burnished wrack burns in yon western sky."

Then she was quiet so that no single word should fall to ripple the clear surface of her joy. The pepper tree rustled; there was a little stir in the leaves of the bougain-villaea. From the ocean, twenty miles away, the sea air was beginning to move back across the land. "It is as good against the dry face as water." She pushed her crackling hair away from her cheeks. "I won't have a windbreak as thin even as one hair against my face."

She arched her chest under the tightly wrapped lace scarf, so that she could project as much of herself as possible into the evening's beauty. "Now the sun is down and the day's long dream ended. Now I must make the air whistle about my ears."

She came out of the long black lace scarf like an ivory crucifix—with a body scarcely wider than her arms. Panties, slip, green rep dress on, and there she was—a girl of twelve again, and the supper to get, and the house to clean. She had the supper in her mind: a fitting meal for Sunday evening. Oyster soup. Oysters that actresses ate, floating in a golden sea of milk, and marble cupcakes veined like old temples for dessert.

She had supper ready when the car turned into the

driveway bringing her family home from their drive—the cakes out of the oven, the milk just on for the soup.

"Well," said Mr. Delahanty when he entered the room, "this is pretty nice." He walked over and held his hands to the fire. "Woodbox full, too."

Her mother ran her finger over the top of the bookcase while she unwound her veil. "Cress, you'll burn us out dusting with kerosene."

Cress watched the scarlet accordion pleating in the opening of her mother's slit skirt fan out, as she held her foot toward the fire.

Father took Mother's coat. "You should have gone with us, Cress. The wind's done a lot of damage over in Riverside County. Lost count of the roofs off and trees down."

"Is supper ready?" Mother asked.

"Soon as the milk heats, and I put the oysters in."

"Oyster soup," exclaimed Father, "the perfect dish for a Sunday October evening. Did you get your studying done?" he asked curiously.

Cress nodded. Studying. Well, it was studying. There were her books and papers.

Father had said that morning before they left, "You're a bright girl, Cress. No need your spending a whole day studying. Do you more good to go for a ride with us."

"No, Father, I'm way behind." She could hardly wait until they left.

Finally at ten they got into the car, Mother on the front seat close to Father. Father backed out of the driveway and a dusty swirl of wind caught Mother's scarlet veil. They waved her a sad good-by.

She had watched the red car out of sight, then she turned and claimed the empty house for herself.

She was as happy as a snail that expels the last grain of sand which has separated its sensitive, fluid body from its shell. Now she flowed back against the walls of her house in pure contentment. She stood stock still and shut her eyes and listened to the house sounds: first the dry, gusty breathing of the wind and the shingle's tap, then the lessening hiss of the tea kettle as the breakfast fire died, and the soft, animal pad of the rug as a slackening air current let it fall.

She opened her eyes. In the dining room the curtains lifted and fell with a summer movement in the autumn wind. She felt this to be perfect happiness: to stand in one room and watch in another the rise and fall of curtains. The egg-rimmed dishes still stood on the uncleared breakfast table. She regarded the disorder happily. "Oh," she whispered, "it's like being the only survivor on an abandoned ship."

Stealthily she ran to lower all the blinds so that the room was left in yellow, dusty twilight. Then she made herself a fire of the petroleum-soaked refuse from the oil fields that they used for wood. When the oil began to bubble and seethe, and the flames darted up, black and red, she started her work.

She cleared the fumed oak library table and ranged her books and papers precisely before her. Now her day began.

Now she inhabited two worlds at once, and slid amphibian-like from one to the other, and had in each the best. Mist-like she moved in Shelley's world of luminous mist, and emerged to hold her hand to the fire and to listen to the bone-dry sound of the wind in the palm trees.

She laid her hand across her open book feeling that the words there were so strong and beautiful that they would enter her veins through her palms and so flow to her heart. She listened to the wind and saw all the objects that bent before it: she saw the stately movement of dark tree tops, the long ripple of bleached, hair-like grass, the sprayed sea water, the blown manes of horses in open pasture, the lonely sway of electric signs along dusty main streets. "Far across the steppes," she said, "and the prairie lands, the high mesas and the grass-covered pampas." She watched the oil bubble stickily out of the wood and wondered what it was like to feel again after these thousands of years the touch of the wind.

But this was dreaming, not doing her work. She opened her notebook to a half-filled page, headed: "Beautiful, Lilting Phrases from Shelley." The list slid across her tongue like honey: "Rainbow locks, bright shadows, riven waves, spangled sky, aery rocks, sanguine sunrise, upward sky, viewless gale." She felt the texture of the words on her fingers as she copied them. The shingle tapped, the wind blew grittily across the pane, the fire seethed.

She finished Shelley and started on her own word list. She was through with the o's, ready to begin on the p's. She opened her old, red dictionary. What words would

she find here? Beautiful, strange ones? She looked ahead—
pamero: a cold wind that sweeps over the pampas; *pars-*
alene: a mock moon; *panada:* bread crumbs boiled in milk;
picaroon: a rogue; *pilgarlic:* a bald-headed man; *plangent:*
resounding like a wave. Her eyes narrowed regarding this
rich store.

She rolled her bobby socks up and down, back and forth
over across her ankles and copied words and definitions.
When she finished the q's she put her word notebook away
and took out one called "The Poems of Crescent Delahanty, Volume III." Each Sunday she copied one poem
from her week's output into her poem book. Her poems
were nothing like Shelley's. Shelley was beautiful, but he
was not a modern. Cress was a modern, and when she
wrote poetry she scorned the pretty and euphonious. This
week's poem was called, "You Do Not Have to Wipe the
Noses of Your Dreams," and Cress thought it as stark and
brutal as anything she had ever done. Slowly she copied it:

> *I was lithe and had dreams;*
> *Now I am fat and have children.*
> *Dreams are evanescent*
> *Dreams fade.*
> *Children do not.*
> *But then you do not have to*
> *Wipe the noses of your dreams.*

"Yes," she said to her father, having remembered the
poems, hers and Shelley's, the long lists of words, "I finished my studying all right."

"Did anyone come while we were gone?" Mother asked.

"Mrs. Beal knocked, but she left before I got to the door."

She had scarcely moved from her table all morning. Now her back was stiff; she was cold and hungry. She put another petroleum-soaked timber on the fire and sat on the hassock, warming her knees and eating her lunch: a mixture of cocoa, sugar, and condensed milk as thick and brown as mud. She spooned it from gravy bowl to mouth and watched the murky flames and listened to the block of wood which was burning as noisily as a martyr. The oil seethed and bubbled like blood. She crouched on the hearth and heard behind the drawn curtains the hiss of sand against the windows. A current of air like a cold finger touched her cheek.

"What do I here," she wondered, "alone, abandoned, hiding?"

She pressed herself closely against the bricks and listened intently. She took a bite and let the sweet, brown paste slide down her throat so that no sound of swallowing should mask the approaching footfall, the heavy, guarded breathing. The room was filled with a noiseless activity. Well, she had known this would be her end. Soon or late they would come, search her out. In some such sordid, dirty, ill-lit hole as this she had been destined to make her end.

"In solitude and from this broken crockery the, this last meal," she mused, and looked scornfully at the cracked bowl. "And those for whom the deed was done eat from crystal, on linen napery, and talk with light voices."

The wind had died down. But the curtains moved stealthily and the door into the hallway trembled a little in its frame. From somewhere in the house came the light click, click of metal on metal. Light, but continuous. She had not heard it before. Her cheekbones ached with the intensity of her listening. She shifted her weight cautiously on the hassock so that she faced the room.

The wind came up again with a long, low, sick whistle; the shingle beat feverishly. She put down her bowl and started the search she knew must be made. She stepped out of her shoes and noiselessly opened the door into the hall. Cold, dark, and windowless it stretched the length of the house. Three bedroom doors opened off it, two to the west, one to the east. She searched the bedrooms carefully, though her heart-beat jarred her cheeks. She lunged against the long, hanging garments that might have concealed a hidden figure. She threw back the covers from the unmade beds. She watched the mirrors to see if from their silver depths a burning, red-rimmed eye might look into hers.

In the spare bedroom she finished her search. The loose shingle tapped like the heart of a ghost. Then she heard it; the sound she had been born to hear, the footstep her ears had been made to echo. Furtive footsteps: now fast, now slow, now pausing altogether. She leaned against the side of the dressing table and waited for the steps to turn toward the house.

"But how could they know this was the house? What sign did I leave? What clue not destroy?"

The footsteps came on inexorably, turned out of the road onto the graveled walk then proceeded quickly and resolutely to the front door. First there was a light, insistent knock, then the latched screen door was heavily shaken.

"He must have come in force," Cress thought, "he is so bold," and she waited for the crash of splintering boards, and braced her body for the thrust of cold steel that would follow. She thought fleetingly of her father and mother, and wondered if any sudden coldness about their hearts warned them of her plight.

The screen door shook again, and a woman's voice, old and quiet, called out, "Is there anyone there? I say, is there anyone home?" and ceased.

Slowly, cautiously Cress crept to the living room, lifted the side of the green blind. Old Mrs. Beal, her Sunday black billowing in the wind, was homeward bound from dinner with her daughter.

"I saw it was old Mrs. Beal on her way home from her daughter's," she told her father, giving her father as much truth as she thought he could handle.

"Cress, you can get to the door fast enough when some of your friends are calling."

"I was busy," replied Cress with dignity. Her father looked at her doubtfully, but said no more.

Her mother combed out her bangs with her rhinestone

back comb. "Did you forget to feed Brownie?" she asked.

"Of course I fed Brownie. I'll never forget her. She's my dearest friend."

Against the warm reality of Mrs. Beal's broad home-ward-bound back, the world that had been cold and full of danger dissolved. The dear room; her books, her papers; Mother's tissue cream on top of the piano; the fire send-ing its lazy red tongue up the chimney's black throat.

She stood warming herself, happy and bemused, like a prisoner unexpectedly pardoned. Then she heard again the click, click she had not recognized. Brownie at the back door!

"Oh, poor Brownie, I forgot you. Poor kitty, are you hungry?" There was Brownie sitting on the back step, with fur blown and dusty, patiently waiting to be let in and fed. She was a young cat, who had never had a kit of her own, but she looked like a grandmother. She looked as if she should have a gingham apron tied around her waist, and spectacles on her nose, and now out of her grandmother's eyes she gave Cress a look of tolerance. Cress snatched the cat up and held her close to her face, and rubbed her nose in the soft, cool fur. When she got out the can of evaporated milk she sat Brownie by the fire and poured the milk into the bowl from which she had eaten her own lunch. Brownie lapped the yellow arc as it fell from can to bowl.

Cress crouched on the hearth with her eyes almost on a level with Brownie's. It was blissful, almost mesmeric to watch the quick, deft dart of the red tongue into the yellow milk. Her own body seemed to participate in that darting, rhythmic movement and was lulled and happy. "It is almost as if she rocked me, back and forth, back and forth, with her tongue," mused Cress.

When Brownie finished eating, Cress took her in her arms, felt the soft, little body beneath the shaggy envelope of cinnamon fur. She lay on the floor close to the fire and cradled Brownie drowsily. Suddenly she kissed her. "My darling, my darling," she said and caressed the cat the length of its long soft body. Her hand tingled a little as it passed over the little pin-point nipples.

Some day her mother would tell her the secret phrase, the magic sentence—something the other girls already knew. Then the boys would notice her. Then he would come. Jo and Ina and Bernadine already had notes from boys, and candy hearts on Valentine's day, and a piece of mistletoe at Christmas time. The boys rode them on their handlebars and showed them wrestling holds, and treated them to sodas. "But no one," she mourned, "ever looks at me." She pressed her apricot-colored hair close to the cat's cinnamon fur. "It's because Mother hasn't told me yet. Something the other girls know. Sometime she'll tell me— some beautiful word I've been waiting a long time to hear. Then I'll be like a lamp lighted, a flower bloomed. Maybe she'll tell me tomorrow—and when I walk into school everyone will see the change, know I know. How will they know? My lips, my eyes, a walk, a gesture, the movement of my arms. But there's not a boy here I'd have, but someone far away, no boy. He will come and we will walk out along the streets hand in hand and everyone will see us and say, 'They were made for each other.' His hair will be like fur, soft and sooty black, and on his thin brown cheek will be a long, cruel scar. He will say, 'Kiss it, Cress, and I will bless the man who did it.' Ah, we shall walk together like sword and flower. All eyes will follow us and the people will say, 'This is Cress. Why did we never see her before.' "

Fire and wind were dying. Brownie slept on her arm. "He will come, he will come." Cress lifted Brownie high overhead, then brought her down sharply and closely to her breast.

"He will come, he will come." She kissed Brownie fiercely and put her on the floor, and ran to her mother's room, undressing as she went. She stepped out of her skirt and threw her jacket and sweater across the room and sent her panties in a flying arc. She knew what she wanted. She had used it before—Mother's long, black lace shawl. She wound it tightly about herself from armpits to thighs. She unbraided her hair and let it hang across her shoulders. Then she turned to the mirror. "I have a beautiful body," she breathed, "a beautiful, beautiful body."

And because she regarded herself, thinking of him, he who was yet to come, it was as if he too, saw her. She loaned him her eyes so that he might see her, and to her flesh she gave this gift of his seeing. She raised her arms and slowly turned and her flesh was warm with his seeing. Somberly and quietly she turned and swayed and gravely touched now thigh, now breast, now cheek, and looked and looked with the eyes she had given him.

She moved through the gray dust-filled room weaving an ivory pattern. Not any of the dust or disorder of her mother's room fazed her, not its ugliness nor funny smell. Hair bubbled out of the hair receiver, the stopper was out of the cologne bottle, the mirror was spattered with liquid powder. She made, in her mind, a heap of all that was ugly and disordered. She made a dunghill of them and from its top she crowed.

"The curtains, green as vomit, and hanging crooked, the gray neckband on the white flannel nightgown, the dust on the patent leather shoes," she said, providing her imaginary stage with imaginary props, "I hate them and dance them down. Nothing can touch me. I am Cress. Or I can dance *with* them," she said and she clasped the nightgown to her and leaped and bent. "This is evil, to be naked, to like the feel of gritty dust under my feet, the bad smell, the dim light."

She regarded her face more closely in the spattered mirror. "There is something wanton and evil there," she thought, "something not good. Perhaps I shall be faithless," and she trembled with pity for that dark one who loved her so dearly. She shook back her hair and pressed her cool hands to her burning cheeks and danced so that the dust motes in the slanting shaft of light shot meteorlike, up and down.

"I can dance the word," she whispered, "but I cannot say it." So she danced it, wrapped in the black shawl, with

the dust motes dancing about her. She danced it until she
trembled and leaning on bent elbows looked deep into the
mirror and said, "There is nothing I will not touch. I am
Cress. I will know everything."

All at once she was tired. She turned and walked slowly
to the living room. Brownie lay by the dead fire. "I,
Cress," she had said, "in the October day, in the dying
October day," and turned to do the evening work.

"If the milk boils, your soup will be spoiled," Mother
said. "We've been here long enough for it to heat."

"Yes, sister, let's eat," said Father, "it's been a long
day."

"Yes, let's eat," cried Cress. "It's been a long, beautiful
day," and she ran to the kitchen to put the oysters in the
milk.

Winter

While her mother and father awaited the arrival of Mr. and Mrs. Kibbler who had called asking to speak to them "about Cress and Edwin Jr.," Mr. Delahanty reminded his wife how wrong she had been about Cress.

"Not two months ago," he said, "in this very room you told me you were worried because Cress wasn't as interested in the boys as a girl her age should be. In this very room. And now look what's happened."

Mrs. Delahanty, worried now by Mrs. Kibbler's message, spoke more sharply than she had intended. "Don't keep repeating, 'in this very room,'" she said, "as if it would have been different if I'd said it in the back porch or out of doors. Besides, what has happened?"

Mr. Delahanty took off his hat, which he'd had on when Mrs. Kibbler phoned, and sailed it out of the living room toward the hall table, which he missed. "Don't ask me what's happened," he said, "I'm not the girl's mother."

Mrs. Delahanty took off her own hat and jabbed the hat pins back into it. "What do you mean, you're not the girl's mother? Of course you're not. No one ever said you were."

Mr. Delahanty picked up his fallen hat, put it on the chair beside the hall table and came back into the living room. "A girl confides in her mother," he told his wife.

"A girl confides in her mother!" Mrs. Delahanty was very scornful. "Who tells you these things, John Delahanty? Not *your* mother. She didn't have any daughter. Not me. Cress doesn't confide in anyone. How do you know these things, anyway, about mothers and daughters?"

John Delahanty seated himself upon the sofa, legs extended, head back, as straight and unrelaxed as a plank.

"Don't catch me up that way, Gertrude," he said. "You know I don't know them." Without giving his wife any opportunity to crow over this victory he went on quickly: "What I'd like to know is why did the Kibblers have to pick a Saturday night for this call? Didn't they know we'd be going into town?"

Like most ranchers, John Delahanty stopped work early on Saturdays so that, after a quick clean-up and supper, he and his wife could drive into town. There they did nothing very important: bought groceries, saw a show, browsed around in hardware stores, visited friends. But after a week of seeing only themselves—the Delahanty ranch was off the main highway—it was pleasant simply to saunter along the sidewalks looking at the cars, the merchandise, the people in their town clothes. This Saturday trip to town was a jaunt they both looked forward to during the week, and tonight's trip, because of February's warmer air and suddenly, it seemed, longer twilight, would have been particularly pleasant.

"Five minutes more," said Mr. Delahanty, "and we'd have been on our way."

"Why didn't you tell Mrs. Kibbler we were just leaving?"

"I did. And she said for anything less important she wouldn't think of keeping us."

Mrs. Delahanty came over to the sofa and stood looking anxiously down at her husband. "John, exactly what did Mrs. Kibbler say?"

"The gist of it," said Mr. Delahanty, "was that . . ."

"I don't care about the gist of it. That's just what you think she said. I want to know what she really said."

Mr. Delahanty let his head fall forward, though he still kept his legs stiffly extended. "What she really said was, 'Is this Mr. John Delahanty?' And I said, 'Yes.' Then she said, 'This is Mrs. Edwin Kibbler, I guess you remember me.' "

"Remember her?" Mrs. Delahanty exclaimed. "I didn't know you even knew her."

"I don't," said Mr. Delahanty, "but I remember her all right. She came before the school board about a month ago to tell us we ought to take those two ollas off the school grounds. She said it was old-fashioned to cool water that way, that the ollas looked messy and were unhygienic."

"Did you take them off?" Mrs. Delahanty asked, without thinking. As a private person John Delahanty was reasonable and untalkative. As clerk of the school board he inclined toward dogmatism and long-windedness. Now he began a defense of the ollas and the school board's action in retaining them.

"Look, John," said Mrs. Delahanty, "I'm not interested in the school board or its water coolers. What I want to know is, what did Mrs. Kibbler say about Cress?"

"Well, she said she wanted to have a little talk with us about Cress—and Edwin Jr."

"I know that." Impatience made Mrs. Delahanty's voice sharp. "But what about them?"

Mr. Delahanty drew his feet up toward the sofa, then bent down and retied a shoelace. "About what Cress did to him—Edwin Jr."

"*Did* to him!" said Mrs. Delahanty aghast.

"That's what his mother said."

Mrs. Delahanty sat down on the hassock at her husband's feet. "Did to him," she repeated again. "Why, what could Cress do to him? He's two or three years older than Cress, fifteen or sixteen anyway. What could she do to him?"

Mr. Delahanty straightened up. "She could hit him, I guess," he ventured.

"Hit him? What would she want to hit him for?"

"I don't know," said Mr. Delahanty. "I don't know that she did hit him. Maybe she kicked him. Anyway, his mother seems to think the boy's been damaged in some way."

"Damaged," repeated Mrs. Delahanty angrily. "Damaged! Why, Cress is too tender-hearted to hurt a fly. She shoos them outside instead of killing them. And you sit there talking of hitting and kicking."

"Well," said Mr. Delahanty mildly, "Edwin's got teeth out. I don't know how else she could get them out, do you?"

"I'm going to call Cress," said Mrs. Delahanty, "and ask her about this. I don't believe it for a minute."

"I don't think calling her will do any good. She left while I was talking to Mrs. Kibbler."

"What do you mean, left?"

"Went for a walk, she said."

"Well, teeth out," repeated Mrs. Delahanty unbelievingly. "Teeth out! I didn't know you could get teeth out except with pliers or a chisel."

"Maybe Edwin's teeth are weak."

"Don't joke about this, John Delahanty. It isn't any joking matter. And I don't believe it. I don't believe Cress did it or that that boy's teeth are out. Anyway I'd have to see them to believe it."

"You're going to," Mr. Delahanty said. "Mrs. Kibbler's bringing Edwin especially so you can."

Mrs. Delahanty sat for some time without saying anything at all. Then she got up and walked back and forth in front of her husband, turning her hat, which she still held, round and round on one finger. "Well, what does Mrs. Kibbler expect us to do now?" she asked. "If they really are out, that is?"

"For one thing," replied Mr. Delahanty, "she expects us to pay for some new ones. And for another . . ." Mr.

Delahanty paused to listen. Faintly, in the distance, a car could be heard. "Here she is now," he said.

Mrs. Delahanty stopped her pacing. "Do you think I should make some cocoa for them, John? And maybe some marguerites?"

"No, I don't," said Mr. Delahanty. "I don't think Mrs. Kibbler considers this a social visit."

As the car turned into the long driveway which led between the orange grove on one side and the lemon grove on the other to the Delahanty house, Mrs. Delahanty said, "I still don't see why you think this proves I'm wrong."

Mr. Delahanty had forgotten about his wife's wrongness. "How do you mean wrong?" he asked.

"About Cress's not being interested in the boys."

"Oh," he said. "Well, you've got to be pretty interested in a person—one way or another—before you hit him."

"That's a perfectly silly notion," began Mrs. Delahanty, but before she could finish, the Kibblers had arrived.

Mr. Delahanty went to the door while Mrs. Delahanty stood in the back of the room by the fireplace unwilling to take one step toward meeting her visitors.

Mrs. Kibbler was a small woman with a large, determined nose, prominent blue eyes and almost no chin. Her naturally curly hair—she didn't wear a hat—sprang away from her head in a great cage-shaped pompadour which dwarfed her face.

Behind Mrs. Kibbler was Mr. Kibbler, short, dusty, soft-looking, bald, except for a fringe of hair about his ears so thick that the top of his head, by contrast, seemed more naked than mere lack of hair could make it.

Behind Mr. Kibbler was Edwin Jr. He was as thin as his mother, as mild and soft-looking as his father; and to these qualities he added an unhappiness all of his own. He gave one quick look at the room and the Delahantys through his thick-lensed spectacles, after which he kept his eyes on the floor.

Mr. Delahanty closed the door behind the callers, then introduced his wife to Mrs. Kibbler. Mrs. Kibbler in turn introduced her family to the Delahantys. While the Kibblers were seating themselves—Mrs. Kibbler and Edwin Jr. on the sofa, Mr. Kibbler on a straight-backed chair in the room's darkest corner—Mrs. Delahanty, out of nervousness, bent and lit the fire, which was laid in the fireplace, though the evening was not cold enough for it. Then she and Mr. 'Delahanty seated themselves in the chairs on each side of the fireplace.

Mrs. Kibbler looked at the fire with some surprise. "Do you find it cold this evening, Mrs. Delahanty?" she asked.

"No," said Mrs. Delahanty, "I don't. I don't know why I lit the fire."

To this Mrs. Kibbler made no reply. Instead, without preliminaries, she turned to her son. "Edwin," she said, "show the Delahantys what their daughter did to your teeth."

Mrs. Delahanty wanted to close her eyes, look into the

fire, or find, as Edwin Jr. had done, a spot of her own on the floor to examine. There was an almost imperceptible ripple along the length of the boy's face as if he had tried to open his mouth but found he lacked the strength. He momentarily lifted his eyes from the floor to dart a glance into the dark corner where his father sat. But Mr. Kibbler continued to sit in expressionless silence.

"Edwin," said Mrs. Kibbler, "speak to your son."

"Do what your mother says, son," said Mr. Kibbler.

Very slowly, as if it hurt him, Edwin opened his mouth.

His teeth were white, and in his thin face they seemed very large, as well. The two middle teeth, above, had been broken across in a slanting line. The lower incisor appeared to be missing entirely.

"Wider, Edwin," Mrs. Kibbler urged. "I want the Delahantys to see exactly what their daughter is responsible for."

But before Edwin could make any further effort Mrs. Delahanty cried, "No, that's enough."

"I didn't want you to take our word for anything," Mrs. Kibbler said reasonably. "I wanted you to see."

"Oh, we see, all right," said Mrs. Delahanty earnestly.

Mr. Delahanty leaned forward and spoke to Mrs. Kibbler. "While we see the teeth, Mrs. Kibbler, it just isn't a thing we think Crescent would do. Or in fact how she *could* do it. We think Edwin must be mistaken."

"You mean lying?" asked Mrs. Kibbler flatly.

"Mistaken," repeated Mr. Delahanty.

"Tell them, Edwin," said Mrs. Kibbler.

"She knocked me down," said Edwin, very low.

Mrs. Delahanty, although she was already uncomfortably warm, held her hands nearer the fire, even rubbed them together a time or two.

"I simply can't believe that," she said.

"You mean hit you with her fist and knocked you down?" asked Mr. Delahanty.

"No," said Edwin even lower than before. "Ran into me."

"But not on purpose," said Mrs. Delahanty.

Edwin nodded, "Yes," he said. "On purpose."

"But why?" asked Mr. Delahanty. "Why? Cress wouldn't do such a thing, I know—without some cause. Why?"

"Tell them why, Edwin," said his mother.

Edwin's head went even nearer the floor—as if the spot he was watching had diminished or retreated.

"For fun," he said.

It was impossible not to believe the boy as he sat there hunched, head bent, one eyelid visibly twitching. "But Cress would never do such a thing," said Mrs. Delahanty.

Mrs. Kibbler disregarded this. "It would not have been so bad, Mr. Delahanty, except that Edwin was standing by one of those ollas. When your daughter shoved Edwin over she shoved the olla over, too. That's probably what broke his teeth. Heavy as cement and falling down on top of him and breaking up in a thousand pieces. To say nothing of his being doused with water on a cold day. And Providence alone can explain why his glasses weren't broken."

"What had you done, Edwin?" asked Mrs. Delahanty again.

"Nothing," whispered Edwin.

"All we want," said Mrs. Kibbler, "is what's perfectly fair. Pay the dentist's bill. And have that girl of yours apologize to Edwin."

Mrs. Delahanty got up suddenly and walked over to Edwin. She put one hand on his thin shoulder and felt him twitch under her touch like a frightened colt.

"Go on, Edwin," she said. "Tell me the truth. Tell me why."

Edwin slowly lifted his head. "Go on, Edwin," Mrs. Delahanty encouraged him.

"He told you once," said Mrs. Kibbler. "Fun. That girl of yours is a big, boisterous thing from all I hear. She owes my boy an apology."

Edwin's face continued to lift until he was looking directly at Mrs. Delahanty.

He started to speak—but had said only three words, "Nobody ever wants," when Cress walked in from the hall. She had evidently been there for some time, for she went directly to Edwin.

"I apologize for hurting you, Edwin," she said.

Then she turned to Mrs. Kibbler. "I've got twelve

seventy-five saved for a bicycle. That can go to help pay for his teeth."

After the Kibblers left, the three Delahantys sat for some time without saying a word. The fire had about died down and outside an owl, hunting finished, flew back toward the hills, softly hooting.

"I guess if we hurried we could just about catch the second show," Mr. Delahanty said.

"I won't be going to shows for a while," said Cress.

The room was very quiet. Mrs. Delahanty traced the outline of one of the bricks in the fireplace.

"I can save twenty-five cents a week that way. Toward his teeth," she explained.

Mrs. Delahanty took the poker and stirred the coals so that for a second there was an upward drift of sparks; but the fire was too far gone to blaze. Because it had not yet been completely dark when the Kibblers came, only one lamp had been turned on. Now that night had arrived the room was only partially lighted; but no one seemed to care. Mr. Delahanty, in Mr. Kibbler's dark corner, was almost invisible. Mrs. Delahanty stood by the fireplace. Cress sat where Edwin had sat, looking downward, perhaps at the same spot at which he had looked.

"One day at school," she said, "Edwin went out in the fields at noon and gathered wild flower bouquets for everyone. A lupine, a poppy, two barley heads, four yellow violets. He tied them together with blades of grass. They were sweet little bouquets. He went without his lunch to get them fixed, and when we came back from eating there was a bouquet on every desk in the study hall. It looked like a flower field when we came in and Edwin did it to surprise us."

After a while Mr. Delahanty asked, "Did the kids like that?"

"Yes, they liked it. They tore their bouquets apart," said Cress, "and used the barley beards to tickle each other. Miss Ingols made Edwin gather up every single flower and throw it in the wastepaper basket."

After a while Cress said, "Edwin has a collection of bird feathers. The biggest is from a buzzard, the littlest from a hummingbird. They're all different colors. The brightest is from a woodpecker."

"Does he kill birds," Mr. Delahanty asked, "just to get a feather?"

"Oh, no!" said Cress. "He just keeps his eyes open to where a bird might drop a feather. It would spoil his collection to get a feather he didn't find that way."

Mr. Delahanty sighed and stirred in his wooden chair so that it creaked a little.

"Edwin would like to be a missionary to China," said Cress. Some particle in the fireplace as yet unburned, blazed up in a sudden spurt of blue flame. "Not a preaching missionary," she explained.

"A medical missionary?" asked Mr. Delahanty.

"Oh, no! Edwin says he's had to take too much medicine to ever be willing to make other people take it."

There was another long silence in the room. Mrs. Delahanty sat down in the chair her husband had vacated and once more held a hand toward the fire. There was just enough life left in the coals to make the tips of her fingers rosy. She didn't turn toward Cress at all or ask a single question. Back in the dusk Cress's voice went on.

"He would like to teach them how to play baseball."

Mr. Delahanty's voice was matter-of-fact. "Edwin doesn't look to me like he would be much of a baseball player."

"Oh he isn't," Cress agreed. "He isn't even any of a baseball player. But he could be a baseball authority. Know everything and teach by diagram. That's what he'd have to do. And learn from them how they paint. He says some of their pictures look like they had been painted with one kind of bird feather and some with another. He knows they don't really paint with bird feathers," she explained. "That's just a fancy of his."

The night wind moving in off the Pacific began to stir the eucalyptus trees in the windbreak. Whether the wind blew off sea or desert, didn't matter, the long eucalyptus leaves always lifted and fell with the same watery, surf-like sound.

"I'm sorry Edwin happened to be standing by that olla," said Mr. Delahanty. "That's what did the damage, I suppose."

"Oh, he had to stand there," said Cress. "He didn't have any choice. That's the mush pot."

"Mush pot," repeated Mr. Delahanty.

"It's a circle round the box the olla stands on," said

Crescent. "Edwin spends about his whole time there. While we're waiting for the bus anyway."

"Crescent," asked Mr. Delahanty, "what is this mush pot?"

"It's prison," said Cress, surprise in her voice. "It's where the prisoners are kept. Only at school we always call it the mush pot."

"Is this a game?" asked Mr. Delahanty.

"It's dare base," said Crescent. "Didn't you ever play it? You choose up sides. You draw two lines and one side stands in the middle and tries to catch the other side as they run by. Nobody ever chooses Edwin. The last captain to choose just gets him. Because he can't help himself. They call him the handicap. He gets caught first thing and spends the whole game in the mush pot because nobody will waste any time trying to rescue him. He'd just get caught again, they say, and the whole game would be nothing but rescue Edwin."

"How do you rescue anyone, Cress?" asked her father.

"Run from home base to the mush pot without being caught. Then take the prisoner's hand. Then he goes free."

"Were you trying to rescue Edwin, Cress?"

Cress didn't answer her father at once. Finally she said, "It was my duty. I chose him for our side. I chose him first of all and didn't wait just to get him. So it was my duty to rescue him. Only I ran too hard and couldn't stop. And the olla fell down on top of him and knocked his teeth out. And humiliated him. But he was free," she said. "I got there without being caught."

Mrs. Delahanty spoke with a great surge of warmth and anger. "Humiliated him! When you were only trying to help him. Trying to rescue him. And you were black and blue for days yourself! What gratitude."

Cress said, "But he didn't want to be rescued, Mother. Not by me anyway. He said he liked being in the mush pot. He said . . . he got there on purpose . . . to observe. He gave me back the feathers I'd found for him. One was a road-runner feather. The only one he had."

"Well, you can start a feather collection of your own," said Mrs. Delahanty with energy. "I often see feathers when I'm walking through the orchard. After this I'll save them for you."

"I'm not interested in feathers," said Cress. Then she added, "I can get two bits an hour any time suckering trees for Mr. Hudson or cleaning blackboards at school. That would be two fifty a week at least. Plus the twelve seventy-five. How much do you suppose his teeth will be?"

"Cress," said her father, "you surely aren't going to let the Kibblers go on thinking you knocked their son down on purpose, are you? Do you want Edwin to think that?"

"Edwin doesn't really think that," Cress said. "He knows I was rescuing him. But now I've apologized—and if we pay for the new teeth and everything, maybe after a while he'll believe it."

She stood up and walked to the hall doorway. "I'm awfully tired," she said. "I guess I'll go to bed."

"But Cress," asked Mrs. Delahanty, "why do you want him to believe it? When it isn't true?"

Cress was already through the door, but she turned back to explain. "You don't knock people down you are sorry for," she said.

After Cress had gone upstairs Mrs. Delahanty said, "Well, John, you were right, of course."

"Right?" asked Mr. Delahanty, again forgetful.

"About Cress's being interested in the boys."

"Yes," said Mr. Delahanty. "Yes, I'm afraid I was."

PART II
Thirteen

Summer I

Grandfather picked up the bowl of pink, white, and red geraniums that Cress had so painstakingly arranged, walked to the kitchen door and gave them, flowers and bowl together, an energetic toss. He was a tall, strong man and Cress heard the bowl splinter against the rocks that bordered the parsley bed at the far end of the yard. Then he went through the kitchen into the sitting room and came back with his accordion. He pushed his chair away from the supper table and his unused plate, sat down, and played two or three chords and then a run of high notes.

"Could I trouble you for a glass, miss?" Mr. Powers asked Cress.

Mr. Powers, Grandfather's hired man, who lived in his own place, a lean-to built against the barn, was eating supper with them this evening by special invitation from Grandfather, though Grandfather himself was not eating. He had come in, had seen the way the table was set and what flowers were on it, and, without a word, had tossed the bowl outside. And now he was evidently going to play his accordion, perhaps even sing, and either seemed terrible to Cress.

"And about four tablespoons of water in the bottom of the glass, miss, if it isn't too much trouble," said Mr. Powers.

Cress took a tablespoon from the silver drawer, went to the sink, and started measuring the water into Mr. Powers' glass. It was her duty to be courteous to any guest of her grandfather's, but she did not care for Mr. Powers; he was odd to look at—red, wattled, and grizzled; he frequently laughed when she said something serious; and she believed that except for him, her grandfather would not be behaving in so peculiar and unfeeling a way a few hours after Grandmother's funeral.

"Ah, don't measure it, miss," said Mr. Powers. "You'll give it a taste of medicine, measuring it out in a spoon that way."

Cress, who had the four tablespoonfuls already in the glass, poured them back into the sink, filled the glass by guess to the height it had been filled before, then put it down in front of Mr. Powers.

"That's more like it," said Mr. Powers. "Measurement's a sickening thing at best and worst of all in a drink. A tittle of this and a tottle of that. A man who don't want a drink bad enough to take a chance on the measurement don't deserve it."

He took a bottle from his coat pocket, pulled the cork with his teeth, and, with no pretense of measurement, splashed a part of its contents in with the four tablespoons of water.

"I don't ask you to join me, Hubert," he said, "knowing you never touch the stuff."

"Tonight I'll change my mind," said Cress's grandfather, and, without waiting for the glass that Cress had risen to get, he picked up Mr. Powers' bottle and drank from it.

"Best thing in the world for you," said Mr. Powers.

Cress's grandfather put down the bottle and said, "While you're up, Cress, take off that apron."

Cress untied the apron, which had been her grandmother's, put it back in the apron drawer, and sat down once more at the supper table. And except that she had cried all the tears that were in her that morning and that her mother had told her to be a comfort to her grandfather, she would have put her head down on the table and cried once more.

The clock in the sitting room struck seven. Mr. Powers ate the corn pudding, pickled beets, and fried chicken the neighbors had brought in as cheerfully as though he were at a wedding party; her grandfather had two more drinks from Mr. Powers' bottle and played some more notes on his accordion, though no whole pieces yet. Cress watched the kitchen curtains, with their borders of purple grapes which her grandmother had stenciled on them, lift and fall in the warm evening air; she listened to a mockingbird singing as loudly as if the day were just beginning, and smelled the rich sweetness of the Marshal Niel roses that grew along the driveway outside the kitchen windows.

She had stood in the driveway by the Marshal Niel

bushes while her mother, father, and grandfather, three people reluctant to part, had talked. She had not listened to them but had looked at the sky. It was no longer clear, as it had been in the morning, but was filmed over with a milky haze. A sudden gust of warm wind, coming across the driveway as they stood there, had broken one of the Marshal Niels apart and deposited its petals on the running board of the car, a little pink heap at the base of the fender.

Her father had absently taken some of the petals in his hand. "Come on home with us for a few days," he had said to her grandfather. "Get away from here. That's the sensible thing to do."

But her grandfather had shaken his head. "It's out of the question, John. Thanks just the same."

"Are you sure you want Cress to stay, Father?" her mother had asked. "Will she be of any help to you? She can brush out for you and cook a few simple things, but after all she's only thirteen."

"She'd be company," her grandfather had said.

"Cress," her mother had said, "Cress, are you listening?"

"Yes, Mother, I'm listening," she had said, though she had been trying not to.

"Do you want to stay, Cress? You don't have to, you know. Your grandfather doesn't want you staying and getting homesick and wishing you hadn't. Do you, Father?"

Before her grandfather could speak, and because she was afraid that if she didn't speak quickly, she would show how much she wanted to go home, she had said, "Of course I want to stay. Besides, it's all been decided."

It was after her father and mother were in the car and the engine running that her mother had leaned out to speak to her alone. "Be a comfort to your grandfather, Crescent."

Be a comfort to her grandfather! What comforting did he need, taking drinks from Mr. Powers' bottle and shamefully, Cress thought, playing the beginnings of pieces on his accordion? He had played enough of "When It's Apple Blossom Time in Normandy" for her to recognize it. Mr. Powers recognized it, too.

"I always liked that song, Hubert," he said.

"Spring's the best season of the year," said her grandfather.

"Some people prefer fall," said Mr. Powers.

"Fall can't hold a candle to spring."

"It's a matter of opinion, Hubert."

"Not with me. It's a matter of fact with me. Every good thing that ever happened to me happened in the spring." Her grandfather spoke as if he expected to be disputed, but Mr. Powers did not dispute him. Instead, he emptied some more of his bottle into his glass.

"Do you want four more tablespoons of water, Mr. Powers?" asked Cress politely.

"Three, four," said Mr. Powers. "It don't matter, really."

Cress let what she judged to be three or four tablespoonfuls dribble into the glass from the faucet and re-

turned the glass to Mr. Powers. He tasted the mixture and
nodded approvingly. "No spoon taste this time."

Cress looked away from both men with shame, but particularly she looked away from her grandfather. She did
not like Mr. Powers, but he was no responsibility of hers.
Let him do what he wanted to. This was not a special day
to him, as it was to her grandfather. It was almost dark,
but she did not intend to turn on the lights. If this playing
and drinking and arguing about the seasons of the year was
to go on, let it go on in the dark, as hidden and secret as
possible.

After the car with her father and mother in it had left
the driveway, she had heard its motor for a minute or two,
though the car itself was out of sight. And after its sound
had faded away, a small cloud of yellow dust had hung
above the road down which the car was traveling and which
the orange groves hid. Then there was nothing at all. No
sound. No dust cloud. She and her grandfather were absolutely alone. It was as if a clock that had been furiously
ticking had suddenly run down, and time, which had been
tangled up in its mechanism, had been able at last to escape.
Cress had felt its heavy everlastingness settle down upon
her and her grandfather.

This was the moment, after Cress's parents had left her
behind for a visit, when, in the past, her grandmother had
often said, "Now that we're rid of those two, how about
something good to eat?" as if losing those two were no
occasion for homesickness but something her grandmother,

her grandfather, and herself had looked forward to and could take advantage of with all kinds of treats and feastings.

So when her father and mother had driven off at last, after the funeral, Cress had looked up at her grandfather and said, "How about something good to eat now that we're rid of those two?"

Her grandfather had given a kind of shudder and had bent his head down toward her as if he had just returned from a distance and were surprised to find her beside him.

"Is it time to eat?" he'd said.

"It's time for supper."

"I suppose we have to eat," he had answered. "Call me when you're ready."

She had gone into the kitchen but had not started supper at once. Instead, she had stood for some time in the center of the warm, shadowy room, looking about. It was harder for her to believe that her grandmother was dead than that she was still alive and likely to step into the kitchen at any minute, tying her frilled, supper-getting apron about her waist, saying, "Well, lovey, want to peel some potatoes for me?" And giving her a quick, laughing hug perhaps as she added, "Try to save me a little core of potato for cooking when you peel them, Crescent. A little sliver at the center we can eat."

But tonight the kitchen had remained silent, empty— no voice, no footfall, no movement except the occasional lift and fall of the curtains in the warm air of the summer evening. There had been no real cooking to do. Cress had put the water on for her grandfather's tea, set the corn pudding in the oven to heat, and filled a platter with cold fried chicken. It was a good thing she had filled the platter high, for Mr. Powers was eating now, as he drank, without counting. Cress counted, though. There were already five bones on his plate, and they were not wing bones, either. Mr. Powers saw her eyes counting and said, "It's been some time since I had fried chicken."

Cress stopped looking at Mr. Powers' plate but said nothing.

"I once drove down a road arched over for a quarter of a mile with blossoming lindens," her grandfather said. "Drove it in a horse and buggy. I don't recollect ever again smelling so much sweetness at one time. We turned around and drove the length of it once more, just for the sake of the smell."

"This in the springtime, Hubert?"

Cress turned her mind away from such talk and thought instead of the preparations she had made for this supper. While the water for her grandfather's tea had heated, she had set the table. She had set it as her grandmother would have done, cups and saucers on the left-hand side. Her grandmother had been left-handed and had never been able to convince herself that a table set in this way was not more convenient for everyone. Cress had tied one of her grandmother's frilled aprons about her waist, and then, in order that the room should speak of her grandmother in every possible way, she had picked geraniums and arranged them as her grandmother had always done—first a single circle of white geraniums around the outer edge of the bowl, inside that a double ring of pink, and finally, as the heart of the bouquet, a center knot of deep red. When everything was ready, she had called her grandfather in the very words her grandmother had always used —"Could you spare a few minutes for eating?" He had come in but had not eaten.

And now he was playing another song and Mr. Powers was pushing the bottle once more in his direction. Cress got up, said good night, and quickly ran up the dark stairs to her room.

It was a room that her grandmother had arranged especially for her, a blue-and-white room—blue cornflowers on the white curtains and bordering the white valance that hung from beneath the bedspread, a blue blotter on the white desk, and, above the desk, a handful of peacock feathers tied together with a big loop of blue satin ribbon. At the head of her bed hung a verse that had once belonged to her mother. Cress's grandmother not only had written it but had burned it onto a wooden plaque with a kind of needle she had for such work.

It said:

> *Sleep well, sweet child, and may the night*
> *Prepare you for Eternal Light.*
> *Sleep well, sweet child, and when you pray*
> *Ask God to guide you on your way.*

Cress read it through once again, though she knew it by heart.

She went over to the south window and looked out into the summer night. There was another long quaver from the accordion downstairs, and, hearing it, she unlatched the screen and stepped out, as she had often done before, onto the gentle slope of the roof. She sat down, wiped away her tears, and saw that the film that earlier had covered the sky had disappeared. The moon was shining and the white oil tanks that topped the distant hills were softly luminous. She sat for a long time trying to understand her grandfather, and when she heard the screen behind her creak, she said joyfully, "Grandfather?"

"No," said Mr. Powers. "It's not your grandpa. It's me."

He came cautiously down the roof to where Cress was and sat down. "This is a nice place to set on a summer night," he observed. "A nice view of hill and dale."

"Yes," said Cress, thinking that it had been a nice place until Mr. Powers came out.

"I guess your grandpa, throwing out your flowers after you fixed them so nice, kind of hurt your feelings?"

Cress said nothing.

"You got to always remember with him," said Mr. Powers, "that he's hasty. Act first and think second, that's your grandpa's motto."

"They were *his* flowers," said Cress. "And his bowl. He had a right to throw them out if he wanted to."

Mr. Powers leaned over and scanned Cress's face in the moonlight. "Made you cry, though," he said. "Made you sad."

"I wasn't crying for myself."

"For your grandma?"

"No," said Cress, though she didn't want to talk to Mr. Powers at all. "For him."

"Your grandpa?"

"Yes," said Cress. "Not remembering or caring. Arguing and playing music."

"Oh!" said Mr. Powers. After a little, he added, "Why, Cress, he was talking about your grandma the whole while."

"I heard him," said Cress. "Not wanting to be reminded of her."

Mr. Powers started once or twice to speak, then stopped. Finally, he said, "I once knew a man, a soldier. He come as near being blown to pieces as a man can and still live. That man couldn't even say the word for what had happened to him, let alone look at the places he was wounded. He was hurt too bad."

"My grandfather was never a soldier," said Cress obstinately.

Mr. Powers paid no attention to this. "There was another man, a soldier, got himself a scratch on the arm, nothing to speak of, and he was sliding down his bandages every few minutes to have a look at his hurt, he thought it was so interesting."

Cress gazed, without speaking, across the tops of the moonlit groves.

"You understand what I been saying, Cress? About your grandpa?"

"I don't need anyone to explain my own grandfather to me," said Cress stiffly.

"Well, I suppose not." Mr. Powers got up slowly and awkwardly. "You look more like your grandma every day," he said.

"I don't *forget* her, either," said Cress.

At this, Mr. Powers lifted the screen and stepped inside. "I put you a drumstick and pickled beet on your dresser. I noticed you didn't eat your supper."

"I don't feel like eating, thank you," Cress said, then listened as Mr. Powers went slowly down the stairs. She sat for a long time after he had gone, her cheek resting against her drawn-up knees, her mind, she believed, perfectly empty.

After a while, she got up and climbed back into her room. She picked up the drumstick and pickled beet Mr. Powers had brought her and stood before her window eating them. She could see Mr. Powers in his lean-to, outlined against the glass of the front door, rocking steadily in the chair that her grandmother had given him.

Then, as if he could see her and would think her eating a contradiction of all she had said, she told him, "I'm not forgetting Grandma, Mr. Powers, and I never, never will forget her."

Summer II

It was a hot August morning, Saturday, six-thirty o'clock, and Mr. and Mrs. Delahanty still lingered at the breakfast table. Six-thirty is midmorning for a rancher in summer; but Mrs. Delahanty hadn't finished talking about the hat.

"It's perfectly clear why she wants it," she said.

It wasn't perfectly clear to Mr. Delahanty. Besides, he thought it would be interesting to know what one woman thinks of another's reasons for buying a hat, even though the second is only thirteen and her daughter.

"Why?" he asked.

"Edwin," said Mrs. Delahanty.

Mr. Delahanty put down his coffee which was too hot, anyway, for a hot morning.

"Edwin!" he exclaimed.

"Oh yes," Mrs. Delahanty assured him.

Mr. Delahanty decided to drink his coffee. After drinking, he asked, "How does the hat figure in it?"

"I think Cress thinks this hat would make Edwin see her in a new light. Frail and feminine."

"Better let her have it, hadn't you?" asked Mr. Dela-

hanty. "Not that I like the idea of encouraging Edwin in
any way."

"This hat," Mrs. Delahanty said, "wouldn't encourage anyone. This hat . . . Oh, Cress," she cried, "don't
slip around that way. You gave me a start. What are
you doing up this hour of the day anyway?"

During summer vacation Cress, unless she had projects
of her own afoot, had to be routed from bed.

"I couldn't sleep," she said. She could tell from their
faces that they had been talking about her. "And I wanted
to ask Father something before he went out to work."
She sat down at the table and turned toward her father
as if they were two together, though seated unfortunately
at a table with a stranger. "Can I call the store and tell
them that if they'll hold the hat, you'll come in and look
at it with me when we go to town tonight?"

"I've looked at it, Cress," said her mother.

"Mother," said Cress very sweetly, "I was speaking to
Father. May I?"

"You don't have to ask permission of me, Cress, to
speak to your father."

"Thank you, Mother," said Cress. "May I, Father?"

"Well," said Mr. Delahanty, "I don't suppose there'd
be any harm in taking a look. Would there, Gertrude?
Though you mustn't count on me for any expert advice
about a hat, Cress."

Cress leaned toward her father. "Daddy," she said—
she hadn't called her father Daddy for years but somehow the word seemed right and natural to her this morn-

ing—"Daddy, if you thought a hat was beautiful and becoming, I'd know it was beautiful and becoming. Or if you thought it was ugly and unsuitable, I'd know it was ugly and unsuitable. Do you know what, Daddy," Cress said and leaned toward her father, admiring the philosophic lines which ran, not from his nose to his mouth and which she thought made people look sour, but from his cheek bone to his jaw bone. "Do you know what?"

"No, Cress," said Mr. Delahanty, "I don't. But I'm waiting to be told."

"I think you probably have instinctive taste."

Mrs. Delahanty laughed, quite loud and long for so early in the morning.

Cress looked at her mother with a mingling of shock and disapproval on her face.

"Were you laughing at me or Daddy, Mother?" she asked politely.

"The two of you," said Mrs. Delahanty. "You and your daddy. Your daddy, Cress, can't tell a bonnet from a bushel basket. Not if the basket has a flower on it, anyway."

"Well, Gertrude," said Mr. Delahanty, "I may not be an expert on hats. I grant you that. But I think I know a pretty hat when I see one."

"That's why I want you to see this hat, Daddy," cried Cress. "It's so downright beautiful."

"That hat, Cress," said her mother, "is the most unsuitable object for a girl of thirteen years to put on her head I ever laid my eyes on."

"Just what do you mean by unsuitable, Gertrude?" asked Mr. Delahanty.

"I mean that hat was never intended for a thirteen-year-old girl. It's for an older—woman," concluded Mrs. Delahanty, wasting irony.

Mr. Delahanty poured himself a glass of milk. "You mean it ties under the chin?" he asked. "Or has . . ." he took a drink of milk, visibly running out of what suggested to him the hat of an older woman.

"Or has a black veil?" Cress helped him.

"No," said Mrs. Delahanty, "it hasn't got a black veil and it doesn't tie under the chin. But every single other thing on this earth that hat has got."

"Now, Gertrude," said Mr. Delahanty, "maybe you'd just better tell me what this hat is really like."

Mrs. Delahanty had a musing look in her eyes. "John, do you remember the chamber of commerce dinner last fall? In Santa Ana?"

"I remember we were there."

"Do you remember the table decorations?"

"No," said Mr. Delahanty, "I can't say I remember the table decorations."

"Well, it's a pity you can't, because then you would know what this hat looks like."

Cress did not like the way her mother had of being funny about serious matters. It was objectionable in any-one, in any mature person that is, and particularly so in a mother. When I have a child, Cress thought, I'll be serious and understanding the rest of my days.

"The table decorations," said Mrs. Delahanty reminiscently, "were horns of plenty, made out of straw mats. And out of them came spilling every fruit, grain, and flower ever grown in Orange County. Cress's hat would look right at home on that table."

"Oh Mother!" cried Cress.

"Except," said Mrs. Delahanty, "that those horns of plenty were of natural-colored straw, while this hat . . ." she paused, searching the room for some object with which to compare it, "while this hat," she concluded, "is an indescribable color."

"Oh Mother," cried Cress again. "It isn't. It's flamingo red."

"I've always considered red a nice warm color," said Mr. Delahanty.

"This is the warmest red, if it *is* red," agreed Mrs. Delahanty, "you ever laid eyes on. And its size!" Once again Mrs. Delahanty's eyes searched the kitchen without finding a comparable object. "It's just unbelievable," she said, shaking her head.

"Which all adds up to saying, I gather," said Mr. Delahanty, "that this hat Cress wants is large and flowered. Is that right, Cress? Is that the way it strikes you?"

The way the hat struck Cress was so overwhelming that she felt she might search the whole world over and still not find any word, any comparison which would explain it or the way she felt about it. The hat was summer time. It was deep and broad like summer. It caused soft scallops of shadow, like summer shadows under the densest trees,

to fall across her face. It was like a poem; it was as much,
"The rose is in full bloom, the riches of Flora are lavishly
strown," as though Keats when he wrote had been thinking of it. The person wearing it would be languorous,
gentle, and delicate. Looking at herself in the store mirror
with that hat on, she had heard herself saying to Edwin,
"If you'll be kind enough to give me your arm I think I'd
like to stroll a little before the dew comes out." And she
had seen how she would look, saying that, glancing ap-
pealingly upward at Edwin from under the brim of the
shadow-casting, summery, flower-laden hat.

"Well, Cress?" asked her father.

"Oh, yes!" said Cress. "That's how it strikes me. May
I call the store and say you'll come in tonight to look at
it?"

"There's no rush, is there?" asked Mr. Delahanty.
"Could look Monday as well as tonight, couldn't we?"

"The rush," said Cress, "is because I want it to wear
to the beach tomorrow. That is, if you approve of it,
Daddy."

"What's the idea, Cress?" asked her father. "A hat to
the beach? You usually put on your bathing cap before
we leave the house."

"Tomorrow," said Cress, "I'm not going to go thrash-
ing about in the water. I'm going to walk about and observe."

"You're not going to be able to observe much, Cress,"
said her mother, "with that hat hanging down over your
eyes."

Cress ignored this. "Father, may or may not I call the S.Q.R.? You don't have to promise to buy it or like it. Only to look at it."

"I guess looking never did any harm," said Mr. Delahanty.

"Now you've gone and done it," said Mrs. Delahanty, when Cress had gone.

"Done what?" asked Mr. Delahanty, innocently.

"Promised her that monstrosity. And all in the world she wants it for is to parade around Balboa in it tomorrow hoping Edwin will catch sight of her."

"Is Edwin at Balboa?"

"His family is. And as far as I know they haven't abandoned him."

"I didn't promise to buy the hat," protested Mr. Delahanty. "All I said I'd do was look at it."

Wearing the hat, Cress felt just as she had known she would: gentle and fragile and drooping. Beautiful, too. Running, with it on, would be utterly out of the question. Even sitting with it on had its difficulties, for the hat with its burden of fruits and flowers had to be balanced just so.

"Father," she called from the back seat, "will you please roll up your window? It's blowing my hat."

"Cress," said Mr. Delahanty, "it's at least ninety in here now and I'm not going to roll this window up another inch. We're barely getting enough fresh air to keep us alive as it is."

"It's blowing the flowers off my hat," cried Cress.

"A few will never be missed," said Mr. Delahanty.

Mrs. Delahanty leaned across her husband and rolled up his window.

"How I could signal, if the need suddenly arose, I don't know," Mr. Delahanty told her, "apart from the fact that I'm suffocating right now."

"Nonsense," said Mrs. Delahanty. "Besides we'll be there in a few minutes."

"Steer for me for a minute, will you, Gertrude?" asked Mr. Delahanty. "I want to get out of this coat before I have a heat stroke."

How ridiculous! Cress felt just right. Warm, summery warm, of course, but though the car windows were tightly closed she could feel the freshness of the sea breeze which was bending the brown grass by the roadside, shaking the palm fronds, ruffling the white leghorns' tails up over their backs like untidy skirts. She could smell the strange salt freshness of the sea, the far, non-land scent of its never-quiet water; and suddenly, in a little gap between two brown hills, she saw the sea itself, blue in the hot air, rippling and glinting under the sun like the scales of big silver-blue fish. Cress sighed so deeply with pleasure that her hat rocked unsteadily and she righted it, holding it for a minute with both hands at just the angle which she hoped it would have when Edwin saw her.

Because Edwin would see her, of course. It was impossible to believe that she, having become the owner of the

most beautiful hat, should be in the same town with
Edwin, without his seeing it and her.

After her father parked the car, he got out his own
and her mother's bathing suits; then the two of them
stood for a time looking at her.

"Well, times change," said Mr. Delahanty. "Times
change. I never thought I'd live to see the day, Cress,
when you'd elect to tramp up and down the boardwalk
on a hot day instead of going swimming with us."

"I'm going to walk and observe," said Cress holding
onto her hat which was hard to control in the stiff sea
breeze which was blowing. "I'm getting a little old for
just sporting around in the water."

"Observe," said Mr. Delahanty, seriously regarding
her. "I can only hope, Cress, the shoe won't be too de-
cidedly on the other foot."

"Now, John," said Mrs. Delahanty, and though she
wasn't ordinarily a mother much given to kissing, she
managed to get sufficiently under the brim of Cress's hat
to give her a loving kiss.

"You're all right, Crescent," she said. "That hat's a
little unusual, but I don't know that I'd want a daughter
of mine trigged out like everyone else. Have a good time.
And I hope you see Edwin."

"Oh Mother," said Cress earnestly, for the knowledge
of her mother's understanding was as comforting to her
as confession after sin.

"Run on now," said Mrs. Delahanty.

"We'll meet you at Tiny's at four," said her father, "and have some ice cream before we go home."

At first, Cress was so certain of seeing Edwin that she walked along the boardwalk, really observing and truly, except for the difficulties she had keeping her hat righted, enjoying the sights and smells of the town and the sea. Now and then in front of a plate glass window which served her as mirror she stopped to admire her hat, to get it on straight again and to poke up the stray hairs which kept dangling down from her not very solid kid-curler curls. Her mother had tried to persuade her not to wear a middy and skirt, saying they didn't go well with her hat. She was glad she hadn't listened to her. A middy was a nautical costume, and what, unless you actually went to sea, was more nautical than the shore? And her hat was the heart of summer, and where was the heart of summer to be found if not in August at the beach? No, looking at herself in the plate glass windows she passed, she was very content with what she saw: under the large hat her neck looked slender and reed-like, a blossom's stem; her eyes were shadowed, her entire aspect gentle, and even, she thought, mysterious. She was glad she had worn her high-heeled patent leather pumps, too. They made her teeter a little, but a swaying gait, she thought, suited the day, the hat, and her own personality; besides denying in the sharpest way possible the tomboy she was afraid Edwin thought her, and who would, no doubt, have worn sneakers.

What with observing, keeping her hat on straight, and practicing on occasional strangers the look of melting surprise with which she planned to greet Edwin, the first hour went by quickly. After the quietness of the ranch, where a whole day often passed with no other sounds than her own and her father's and mother's voices, and where the chief diversions, perhaps, were those of digging up a trap-door spider, or freeing a butcher-bird's victim, the sights and sounds of a beach town on a Sunday afternoon were almost too exciting to be borne.

First, there was the strange light touch of the penetrating wind off the sea on her warm inland body. Then there was the constant, half-heard beat of the surf, hissing as it ran smoothly up the sand, thundering as it crashed against the rocks of the breakwater. There were all the smells of salt and seaweed, of fish and water and wind. There were all the human smells too of the hundreds of people who filled the boardwalk: ladies in print dresses smelling like passing gardens; swimmers with their scents of sun-tan oils and skin lotions; there were the smells of the eating places: of mustard and onions, of hamburgers frying; and the sudden sharp smell of stacks of dill pickles, as brisk in the nose as a sudden unintended inhalation of sea water. There was the smell of frying fish from the many fish grottos. And outside these places, in the middle of the boardwalk like miniature, land-locked seas, the glass tanks, where passers-by might admire the grace and color of their dinners before eating them. It was hard to say who did the most looking; fish outward from these sidewalk aquariums, at the strange pale gill-less pedestrians, or pedestrians inward at the finny swimmers.

Cress liked them both. Solemn fish and passers-by, some also solemn, with problems sun and water had not made them forget. For the first hour this was enough for Cress: being a part of this abundance and knowing that at any minute she would see Edwin. For in a town of one street how could she miss him?

Then suddenly the first hour was gone by; it was past three and already the wind seemed a little sharper, the sun less bright, the boardwalk less crowded. More of her hair had come uncurled; her hat took more righting to keep it straight; her neck ached from holding her head high enough to see out from under the hat's brim; occasional stabs of pain shot up the calves of legs unaccustomed to the pull of high heels. A thought, with the swiftness of a stone dropping through water, settled in her mind: he isn't coming. It was a possibility she had not even thought about before. She had thought he would *have* to come. The hat was *for* him. The day was *for* him. How could she possibly, without seeing him, meet her father and mother, say yes, say no, eat ice cream, get in the car, go home, take off her hat, go to bed, sleep?

It was fifteen after three. At first she had been willing that Edwin see her first. Now, she searched every figure, every slight, short man or boy's figure, for as great a distance as she could make them out, saying, "Be Edwin." So strongly did she will it that she thought she might, by determination alone, transform a stranger into Edwin.

It was three-thirty. It was fifteen of four. Her hat was on one side, her mouth weary from practicing her smile on strangers, the pleat out of her freshly starched skirt, her feet mere stumps of pain. Still, she would not give up. "Edwin, appear, Edwin appear," she willed.

Edwin did appear, crossing the street a block away, small and neat and thin in white duck pants and a white shirt. He crossed and turned toward Cress, walking steadily toward her. In two minutes or three he would see her, and see the hat and notice her new gentleness. All tiredness and pain left Cress. She could very easily have flown, or played a piece she had never seen before on the piano, or kissed a mad dog and not been bitten. She had just time to arrange herself, resettle her hat, give her now completely uncurled hair a quick comb upward. To do this she took her hat off, stood on tiptoe, and with fingers which trembled with excitement managed to get it up onto the top of one of the rectangular glass aquariums which by chance stood conveniently before her in the middle of the sidewalk.

Before she, herself, understood what had happened someone was jovially yelling, "Hey, sis, bread crumbs is what you feed them," and there was her hat, slowly, gracefully settling among the startled fish of the aquarium.

The man who had yelled was a short fat man, wearing pants, but no shirt or undershirt. He had sand in the hair on his chest; like dandruff, Cress thought wildly, unable for shame to raise her eyes to his face. "What's the idea, sis?" he asked.

Forcing her eyes away from the sandy dandruff, Cress saw that her hat, still gradually, gracefully floundering, was bleeding flamingo red into the aquarium, so that the amazed fish now swam in sunset waters.

"I thought it had a top," she whispered to no one in particular.

"The hat, sis?" asked the shirtless man.

"The glass place for the fish," Cress whispered. "I thought it had a top."

"It didn't, sis."

"I was resting my hat on it," Cress whispered, "while I fixed my hair."

"You was resting your hat on air, sis."

"It dropped," said Cress. "It fell right out of my hands."

"Gravity, sis," said the fat man. "It was gravity."

"Will it make the fish sick?" asked Cress.

"Make 'em die, sis, in my opinion. Make 'em all puke and throw up their shoestrings I should think."

"What'll I do?" asked Cress.

"Watch 'em die," said the fat man comfortably. "That big one's a goner already."

Cress wanted to die herself. She willed it very hard, but she couldn't. She couldn't even faint, though she held her breath and willed her heart to stop beating. But a sort of numbness did come over her, making all the voices blurred and indistinct, making all the people, and there

were dozens, hundreds it seemed to Cress, now pressed
about the aquarium, distant and hazy.

It was a field day for fish and humans. It was a great
occasion for fish, who had had nothing more exciting to
look forward to than death in the frying pan: a big blunt-
nosed fish swam at the hat as if to ram it; smaller fish circled it curiously; nervous fish parted the darkening waters
in a fishy frenzy. It was a glorious moment for humans,
too, a sight they had never expected to see. Someone, a
worthy man dedicated to service, brought out the fish
grotto proprietor. He came in his white apron and tall
chef's hat, brandishing a long-handled ladle and happy at
first to see his fish arousing so much interest. He shoul-
dered his way through the crowd, his blood-shot eyes
bright with pleasure, until he caught sight of vermilion
waters, frantic fish, and the heart of summer, still partially
afloat among them. He had had a long hard day frying
fish. This was the last straw, fish dying without frying.

"In God's name," he cried, sadly, "who is murdering
my fish?"

Cress was too frightened to reply.

"She is," said the fat man, pointing. "Sis, here, done
it."

"What does she mean?" the fish grotto proprietor cried.
Cress opened her mouth, but not a sound came out. She
was as speechless as the fish.

"Sis here was resting her hat on the top of the aquarium," explained the fat man.

"There ain't no top," said the fish grotto owner. "Is she blind?"

"More or less, I reckon," said the fat man. "You kind of blind, sis?" he asked kindly.

Cress was able only to moan a little. With a long shudder, like a capsized ship coming to rest, her hat settled to the bottom of the aquarium. It lay there at a crazy angle, one side held up by a small castle with which the fish grotto proprietor had attempted to give his aquarium a romantic, gothic air. Out of a castle window one frightened fish eye peered, trying to penetrate the murky waters, make out if this was the end of the world for fish. It looked to be. Flowers and fruits were now adding their colors to that of the flamingo red straw. Streaks of purple from pansies and violets, puffs of sulphurous yellow from the daisies, veins of green from stems and flowers richly marbled the general red of the water. And the hat, in form as well as color, was suffering a sea change. It was softening up, flattening out. Each minute it looked less and less like a hat.

Cress finally found her voice. "Save my hat," she whispered.

"It's too late," the fish grotto proprietor said, "to speak of saving anything. Hat or fishes. They are all goners. Let 'em die together."

"Die?" asked Cress.

"Poisoned," said the fish proprietor, pointing to his frantic fish, the vari-colored water. "What've you got agin fish, kid?"

"I like fish," Cress whispered.

"She likes fish," said the fat man. "Hate to consider what she might do if she didn't." Those who had gathered about the aquarium laughed. Somewhere among them must be Edwin, Cress thought: seeing her, seeing her face trembling with the effort not to cry, seeing her beautiful hat, its colors fading out amongst an aquarium full of fish. The laughter was not malicious; it was lazy Sunday afternoon laughter; lazy Sunday afternoon laughers, watching, as if at play, to see what the fish proprietor would do, if he were villain or hero, straight man or clown. But it might as well have been malicious; it shamed Cress to the bone. It was unthinkable that anyone after such public humiliation could live. She would do nothing wild nor dramatic, simply refuse food, fade quietly away, die.

"Poisoned," declared the fish proprietor again, gloomily, "deliberately poisoned."

"I think you're mistaken about their being poisoned."

It was impossible, Cress thought, that anyone should be defending her: let alone Edwin—Edwin, who was always a victim himself.

"I think that color is probably from pure vegetable dyes," said Edwin. Edwin's face was as white as his shirt and Cress could see that his upper lip trembled. But he was defending her, defying the fish grotto proprietor, not ashamed to be on the side of a person who had been publicly laughed at.

"It might even be good for the fish," suggested Edwin, "that pure vegetable dye."

"Good for them!" cried the fish proprietor. "Them fish have been scared to death at the very least, poison or no poison. Hats descending on them! I wouldn't feed them fish to a cat now. Their nervous systems have been shook up. You related to this girl?"

"No," said Edwin.

"Well, someone," said the fish proprietor, coming to the crux of the matter, "has got to pay for my ruined fish."

"That'll be me, I reckon," said Mr. Delahanty who, without enthusiasm, was pushing his way through the crowd. He took the ladle from the fish owner's hand, and being a tall man was able, by stretching a little, to fetch up the hat, heavy and dripping from the bottom of the aquarium. He held the hat toward Cress, who without a word took it. Then Mr. Delahanty handed the ladle back to its owner.

"I'll pay ten dollars," he said.

"Twenty-five," said the fish grotto proprietor. "Not a cent less. Those were fancy fish and not to be picked up every day in the week."

"Eleven," said Mr. Delahanty.

"I was fond of those fish," said their owner. "They were pets, so to speak."

"Eleven fifty," said Mr. Delahanty.

"It was cruelty to animals putting that hat in with them. I could turn you in to the S.P.C.A."

"Twelve," said Mr. Delahanty.

They settled for fifteen, Mr. Delahanty getting the fish.

Cress, the hat, and the fish, in an oversized kettle loaned by the fish man, occupied the back of the car on the trip home. It was a slow trip because speed tended to slosh the water in the kettle, together with a fish or two, out on the floor. It was a silent trip because Cress was thinking, and because up in the front seat, while Mr. and Mrs. Delahanty had plenty to say, they didn't want to be overheard by Cress.

They were nearly home before Mrs. Delahanty said, very low, "What a terrible thing to happen! It might mark her emotionally for life."

Mr. Delahanty agreed. "It wouldn't have been so bad though if that Edwin hadn't had to turn up in time to see it all."

"I know. She wanted to be such a lady—for him. That hat . . . and the curls . . . and then the hat in with the fish, the curls gone, and all those people laughing. I'm a grown person, John, but I just don't think I could live down such a thing. I think I might just stick my head in that bucket of fish and end everything."

As if her own words had put an idea into her mind, Mrs. Delahanty looked quickly around.

"Cress," she cried, "what have you got that hat on your head for?"

"It'll shrink if I don't," said Cress very calmly.

"Well, let it. Let it shrink. And you've got all those colors dribbling down your face and neck."

"I'm trying to keep them mopped up," said Cress, mopping some more.

"Throw that hat away," ordered Mrs. Delahanty. "Toss it out the window, Cress. You don't ever have to wear it again. We'll get you a new one."

"Oh no," cried Cress, "I love it. I'm going to keep it all my life."

"Keep it all your life?" Mrs. Delahanty asked, feeling rather dazed. "Cress, that hat didn't look too good in the first place. I can't begin to tell you what it looks like now. Throw it away!"

"No," said Cress stubbornly. "I want to keep it to remember today by."

"Remember today," repeated Mrs. Delahanty, who was beginning to feel increasingly that she and her daughter were not speaking of the same day at all. "Why in the world do you want to remember today?"

"Because of the brave way Edwin defended me," said Cress.

"Oh," said Mrs. Delahanty faintly.

"He was really wonderful, Mother. He defied that man."

"I'm afraid we missed that, Cress."

"And I was stricken, Mother, really stricken. It was the first time Edwin ever saw me stricken. He didn't even know I could be. He's always been the stricken one so far.

The most I'd dared hope for was to be gentle. Then," said Cress with great satisfaction, "stricken."

There was complete silence in the car for some time. "Don't you think I was, Mother?" Cress asked anxiously.

"Yes," said Mrs. Delahanty with conviction, "I think that's about the word for it."

"And whenever I wear this hat, he'll remember."

Mrs. Delahanty took her husband's handkerchief from his pocket and handed it back to her daughter. "Tuck this around your neck, Cress. It'll keep those colors from staining your middy."

With one hand Cress tucked the handkerchief about her neck, with the other she kept her hat in place.

Winter I

Mrs. Delahanty went to the door of Crescent's room to remind her that it was time to set the table for supper. It was a fine Saturday afternoon in November and ordinarily Cress would have been outside, up in the hills with friends, or helping her father with the irrigation; or just walking about under the pepper and eucalyptus trees in the yard, deep in a world which found significance in the parchment-like bark peeled from a eucalyptus tree or in a bunch of berries (thirteen berries, exactly the number of years she had been alive—what was the meaning of that?) dropped from the pepper tree. But this afternoon Cress had spent in her room in spite of the clear warm weather and Mrs. Delahanty examined her daughter's stubby, somewhat boyish profile outlined against the golden light of the west windows with considerable curiosity.

"What are you writing, Cress?"

Cress looked up from the sheets of paper spread before her on the drop leaf of the rickety bamboo desk she had bought for herself that summer and said, "I'm not exactly writing, Mother." The sheets had words on them and Cress had a pencil in her hand and, as if aware of this

78

contradiction between appearance and truth, she added, "I'm making a list."

At this Mrs. Delahanty smiled. In school she had learned that ontogeny recapitulates phylogeny and, while she had always been somewhat hazy as to the meaning of that sentence, still it had stayed in her memory and was, amended, her formula for accounting for her daughter: Cress recapitulates John. Since she loved and approved her husband, believing him to be not only handsome but as often as not wise and sensible as well, she was glad this was so. Yet it was strange, as now, to see the gestures and habits of a large dark thirty-five-year-old rancher recapitulated in a medium-sized tow-haired girl.

How much simpler my life would have been, she thought, easing her shoulders against the door jamb, if Cress had recapitulated me, instead of John. John was hard enough to fathom in himself and writ large, without the added need of fathoming a John writ small, condensed, and made more obscure in a daughter. Nor was she helped any in understanding Cress's activity, by the fact that it was one she had witnessed in John for fifteen years. More than fifteen years. She had once broken her engagement for two days because of a list John had made.

John had shown her one evening—with considerable pride, she now realized—a sheet of paper headed in a businesslike way, "Reasons for Loving Gertrude Amboy," a sheet Mrs. Delahanty still remembered with resentment. On it John had analyzed his emotions and her attributes as if both were subjects suitable for the biology textbook

in which she had learned about recapitulation. He had
started out with "I. Character" and wound up with "V.
Physical Beauty," and he had pursued all headings, not
only under A's, B's, and C's but even unto 1's, 2's, and 3's.
It still made her angry, and at the time she had believed
it would be impossible to live with a man capable of dis-
secting his love in so orderly a fashion.

She had thrown his "Reasons for Loving Gertrude
Amboy" down on the floor and stamped on it, treading
with particular energy on the section headed "I. Character,
A. Social, 1. calm." "You haven't an ounce of romance in
your make-up, John Delahanty," she had, she was afraid
now, yelled.

"Gertrude," John had replied, "you know that isn't
true."

She had, too; but she had been really hurt and she had
turned her back on him, though this had been hard to
accomplish, standing as she was with his arms about her,
and had sobbed two or three times.

"I should think you would be glad to know you were
marrying a man of reason," John had defended himself.

She had not said so then, but she thought then, as now,
that there was probably very little connection between
reason and list-making. List-making, she felt sure, was just
a way some people had of being orderly about their unreason. What she had said then was, "A man who could
make a list of reasons for loving anyone, could make a list
for not loving them."

"Could and would," John had acknowledged cheerfully

as though the fact were not damaging. He had held her momentarily far enough away from him to be able to get into his coat pocket. "Look at this," he had said, holding a second sheet across her shoulder. It was headed, "Reasons for Not Loving Gertrude Amboy," and except for "I. None, A. None, 1. None" the sheet was completely empty. Although this, in theory, was just as offensive as the first list, she had not felt quite the same way about it, had in fact been unable to resist kissing John back when he had kissed her. But it had taken her two long miserable days of non-engagement to accommodate herself to the idea of spending a lifetime with a list-maker, and to re-engage herself to John. And little did I know then, she thought, that what I was really going to have to accommodate myself to was a lifetime with two list-makers.

"What are you making a list of, Cress?" she asked.

She had no fear that she was intruding in private matters. One of John's greatest pleasures was the sharing of his lists. After two or three evenings hunched over catalogs and sheets of paper he would look up, about bedtime, and say, "See what you think of this, Gertrude," and begin to read from a list headed, "Supplies Needed for a Prolonged Trip in Sub-Zero Weather." Or perhaps something more simple, as, "The Well-Stocked Cellarette"; or "Minimum Essentials for a Basic Library on Citriculture." They had neither cellar nor cellarette, they lived in Southern California where zero, let alone sub-zero, temperatures were never known, and the essentials of citriculture were all packed away in John's head without need of any library, basic or otherwise.

Cress looked up from *her* list and answered, "I'm making a list of traits, Mother."

"Traits?" Mrs. Delahanty asked.

"Good and bad traits," Cress said, and then explained further. "For school that is."

"You mean personal traits?" Mrs. Delahanty asked.

"Kind of," Cress replied.

Mrs. Delahanty wondered anew. She had never in her life made a list of any kind except a grocery list and this only when pushed into it by John. Life was bigger, and better too, she thought, than words; and it was disappointing and restricting to see a picnic summed up in "Remember Citronella, Kleenex, Band Aid"; or a trip to the city drained of half its promise by a list headed, "Articles Needed En Route." There were clearly two classes of people in the world: those for whom the world was magnified and enriched in words and those who could never find the beautiful world of their living and knowing on any sheet of paper. John and Cress belonged to the first class and she, belonging to the second, could only stand apart, as she did now, trying to understand the need they had for their journals and records, for their "Yesterday I rose at 6:30," and their "Tomorrow I plan to begin rereading *David Copperfield*." And their I's, II's, and III's.

"Traits like honesty, kindness, cheerfulness?" she asked.

"Well, like them," Cress said, "but they aren't on it. This is a list of traits useful for school."

"Isn't honesty useful for school?"

"Nobody at school I ever heard of was popular for honesty," Cress said. After Mrs. Delahanty had considered this in silence for some seconds Cress asked, "Did you ever hear anybody say, 'I'm just crazy about her, she's so honest?' Did you?"

"No," Mrs. Delahanty admitted, "I guess I never did."

"Me either," Cress said. "It's all right to be honest," Cress reassured her, "but there's nothing very outstanding about it."

"Oh I don't know," Mrs. Delahanty said, trying to keep a foothold in this conversation which she felt to be, in spite of its subject matter, pretty slippery. "Look at Diogenes. We've remembered him all these years."

Cress sniffed. "He was hunting for an honest man, not being one. And it was his lantern that was outstanding. That was his trademark. That and his barrel."

"There have been a lot of people with lanterns and barrels we've forgotten, I expect."

Cress agreed. "The trademark's got to stand for something. But if you get a good gag and it stands for something"—for all her conviction of tone Cress looked uncertain—"you're fixed, don't you think?" Before Mrs. Delahanty had answered this—if she could have answered it—Cress asked another question. "Mother, do you think I'm funny?"

"Funny?" Mrs. Delahanty repeated. If Cress was in the midst of some schoolgirl gloom because someone had called her funny, she certainly didn't want to add to it. On the other hand if by funny Cress meant witty she could not truthfully say she wasn't.

"I mean amusing," Cress explained forthrightly. "In your opinion can I say and do amusing things? Can I make you laugh?"

Controlling an inclination to laugh right then Mrs. Delahanty answered, "Yes, Cress. I think you can be very amusing and you have made me laugh many a time."

"Yesterday," Cress said, "I was told very confidentially something Bernadine Deevers said. She said, 'That Crescent Delahanty is deliciously amusing.' It wasn't a trade last or anything like that. I didn't promise Hazel a thing in return for the compliment."

Mrs. Delahanty said, "I don't know about deliciously, but the rest is true enough."

Cress gave her mother a look of awe and unbelieving. "Bernadine Deevers," she said. "Why, I didn't suppose she knew I was alive. Let alone amusing."

"Let alone deliciously," Mrs. Delahanty said, then seeing her daughter's expression alter, doubt replacing radiance, she hurried to add, "Who is this Bernadine, anyway?"

Cress brightened again at once. "Just about the most popular girl in school, that is all. Just about the most outstanding sophomore anyway." Cress herself was a freshman.

"What makes Bernadine so outstanding?"

Cress considered for a while. "Well, Bernadine's got

practically everything, but her trademark is personality."

"Doesn't everyone have personality? Even fathers and mothers?" Mrs. Delahanty asked, trying to be a little amusing herself.

"Everybody has personality," Cress agreed. "Some people have positive personality and some people have negative personality." Mrs. Delahanty waited rather self-consciously for a further development of this idea, but Cress was interested only in Bernadine. "But glamorous personality is Bernadine's trademark."

"How is a person," Mrs. Delahanty asked, with real curiosity, "when a glamorous personality is her trade-mark?"

Mrs. Delahanty had supposed that this question would take some thinking about, but Cress had evidently thought about it before. "When glamorous personality is your trademark you are a law unto yourself," she answered promptly.

Mrs. Delahanty whistled. "Thank goodness your trade-mark isn't personality."

Cress put down her pencil with melancholy finality. "At present," she said, "I don't have a trademark. Not of any kind."

That night after supper Mr. Delahanty, who had been up at five, irrigating, and who was put out with a climate so tardy with its rains that irrigating this late in November was necessary, said to his wife, "I think I'll just stay home and read tonight. I have to reset the water at ten anyway

and we'd have to rush home. You and Cress go ahead
into town if you want to."

"I don't want to go," Cress said. "I'm busy."

"I'm not busy," Mrs. Delahanty admitted, "but I'm not
enough interested in what happens when a lady mayor
meets a male mayor to drive to the movies alone to find
out."

"I can tell you what happens anyway," Mr. Delahanty
said. "Same thing like when lady pearl-diver meets gentle-
man pearl-diver. Or lady surgeon meets male surgeon."

Cress listened to this exchange with an unsmiling face,
then went to her room where Mrs. Delahanty heard the
lid of the bamboo desk at once creak open. The evening
had cooled and at eight Mrs. Delahanty lit a fire of eucalyptus chunks, then challenged her husband to a game of
Russian bank. Mr. Delahanty accepted the challenge but
he did not care whether he won or lost and Mrs. Delahanty wished for Cress, who followed the fall of each card
with the intensity of a player who has the home ranch up
at stake. At nine Cress came out, advised her father to his
benefit on his play, but refused to play herself. "No, I just
came out because of the fire. I've got work to do," she said
and took her papers to the dining-room table.

At nine thirty, after losing his second game, Mr. Delahanty said, "Anybody want to go out and reset the water
for me?" When no one answered he said, "Woman's work
is from sun to sun but man's work is never done," and went
outside cheerfully whistling "Swanee River."

Mrs. Delahanty, who knew what he would want when

he came back to the house, went to the kitchen and made a pot of chocolate and a plate of toasted cheese sandwiches. Cress wandered out, watched her whip the chocolate to a foam and put the sandwiches in the oven, refused anything to eat, then picked up a large wedge of cheese and went off toward her room nibbling gloomily.

Mrs. Delahanty had planned to take the food in by the fire, but Mr. Delahanty said as he pulled off his muddy boots, "Let's have it on the dining-room table where there's room to spread out." He carried the tray in himself and had the chocolate poured by the time Mrs. Delahanty, who had forgotten the napkins, came to the table.

"What's this?" he asked, gesturing with a cheese sandwich toward the sheet of paper beside his chocolate cup.

Mrs. Delahanty, who had an idea, answered only, "What does it say?"

Mr. Delahanty read, stared, drank chocolate and finally said in a voice in which disbelief and sorrowful understanding mingled, "It says here, 'Useful Traits for School. I. Personality, A. Unusual, 1. Witty.'" He put the sheet down. "What's the meaning of this?"

"It's a list," Mrs. Delahanty said. "You ought to understand if anybody would."

Mr. Delahanty ate half a sandwich, then picked up a second sheet. "'My Trademark. Isn't she Crazy!' is the heading here," he said thoughtfully. "'Isn't she Crazy' is in quotes," he explained. "Under it is, 'Useful Gags for Craziness. I. Clothes, A. Shoes, 1. Unmatched.'"

He put the second sheet face down on the first and covered both with the sandwich plate. He finished his cheese sandwich then said, "My God, what a dark world."

"You do understand it, then?" Mrs. Delahanty asked.

"Certainly I understand it. I lived there for a year."

"What year?"

"The year I was thirteen."

Mrs. Delahanty had not known her husband until he was fifteen and these hints of an earlier life always enthralled her. She saw him at thirteen, a big solemn boy with soft dark hair, inquiring eyes, and a sensitive mouth.

"You don't know who you are then, or what you can do. You've got to make a hundred false starts. You've got to make your mark, without knowing what your mark is. Are you a coward or a hero? How do you know without involving yourself in dangerous situations? So you walk ridge poles and visit cemeteries. How do you know you're alive even at that age if you aren't noticed?"

"Dear John," Mrs. Delahanty said. Mr. Delahanty took no notice of this endearment and Mrs. Delahanty hadn't expected him to. He was wound up now, he was back where he had been at thirteen. John Delahanty was the center of Mrs. Delahanty's world. To her mind the light from the fireplace lapped toward him, the rising wind booming in the eucalyptus trees celebrated him, the foothills beyond the orange groves circled around him. John gave her two lives. Without him she would have had only her own life of action, unexamined, not understood. Somebody—John frequently quoted him—had spoken of "the tragedy of an unexamined life"; that, without John, would have been her life and, she supposed, her tragedy. But John, with his eloquent words, yes, they *were* eloquent, she thought, listening now, revealed to her this richer world of motives fully understood and rightly apprehended. By relating the joys and sorrows of his own life to the world's joys and sorrows, past and present, he opened to her depths of meaning which, she felt, her own instinctive living would never have discovered.

"It's the dark time of life," Mr. Delahanty said again. "It turns my stomach now, but at thirteen I too had a trademark."

"A trademark!"

Mr. Delahanty grimaced. "Spitting. At thirteen I was a professional spitter. I used to give exhibitions. Distance and accuracy. Power and control. I had everything. And I hated it. And I still hate anybody now from grammar school days who calls me 'Spit' Delahanty."

"I don't ever remember seeing you spit."

"At fifteen I was far past that, an ex-spitter. By that time I had taken up—" He stopped in mid-sentence. "Cress," he said.

Cress, in her pink sprigged seersucker pajamas, the cheek that had been against the pillow pinker than the other, stood in the opening between living room and dining room. "Did we wake you up with our talk?"

Cress sat down in the chair her father pushed out for her. "No," she said, "you didn't wake me up because I hadn't gone to sleep yet."

Mrs. Delahanty had the feeling that Cress had left her

lists out on purpose, had given them time to read them and would now like to have their opinion of craziness as a trademark. But she was loath to speak of them unless Cress did; and Cress was silent and John went on as if he had never heard of trademarks—or craziness; or spitting, for that matter, either.

"How's school?" Mr. Delahanty asked his daughter. "Classes, teachers, kids? Edwin? Honor Gallagher? Everything turning out as well as you thought it would?"

"Everything's all right," Cress said, opening a cheese sandwich, then closing it like a book she didn't care to read. "Did I tell you I'm probably going to be freshman editor of the year book?"

"No," said Mr. Delahanty, "you didn't. That's fine. Congratulations."

"I'm not editor yet," Cress reminded him.

"But spoken of for the job. Spoken of favorably for the job."

Cress admitted it. "And it's a tradition that the person who is freshman editor is editor in chief his senior year."

"Congratulations," Mr. Delahanty said again; then, shaking the chocolate pot, "Have some cocoa? It's soporific. Just what you need to put you to sleep."

"I read the other day it wasn't," Cress said. "I read it had every bit as much caffein in it as coffee."

"Where? Where'd you read that?"

"In the newspaper."

"The newspaper!" scoffed Mr. Delahanty. "You can read anything in the newspapers. Let's consult the authority." He sprang from his chair with the enthusiasm which the search for a fact always gave him and came back to the table bearing Volume IV of the Britannica, Bishārīn to Calgary. Cress got up and leaned across his shoulder as he flipped the pages. Mrs. Delahanty, while the two of them pursued the word, took the thing itself—caffein or no caffein—to the kitchen to reheat for Cress.

The campaign, "Craziness as a Trademark," seemed to be going well in spite of Mrs. Delahanty's doubts. Cress, as November wore on, had never seemed more happy. Certainly she had never been more active or engrossed—and her activities engaged Mrs. Delahanty's energies as well as her own.

"Life now," Mrs. Delahanty reported to her husband one gray day at lunch, "is very full for me. It is like being property manager for a vaudeville star. It takes a good deal of equipment and thought to achieve the effect of craziness when actually you're as sober as a judge."

"Cress isn't and never was sober as a judge," Mr. Delahanty said. "That Bernadine had something when she said Cress was amusing. Clowning comes naturally to her."

"Not this clowning," Mrs. Delahanty said. "She memorizes lines. She gathers up equipment. She teaches kids their cues. It's exactly as spontaneous as a vaudeville act and I think we ought to put a stop to it."

"How?" Mr. Delahanty asked.

"Just tell her it's silly and to stop it."

"And for the rest of her life she'd blame us for keeping her from finding out who she really was."

"Well, there's no use her finding out the hard way when we could tell her that she suits us just as she is."

"Cress is trying out her wings for a little flight from the us-nest."

"She is trying the wrong wings then, John. Do you know what she did this morning?" Mrs. Delahanty didn't wait for any reply from her husband. "She wore her bedroom slippers to the bus and carried her oxfords. She had to have new bedroom slippers for this, by the way, the old ones wouldn't do for a public appearance. Do you know what the gag is there?"

This time she waited for Mr. Delahanty's answer. "No," he said, "I don't."

"The gag is that she has figured that it takes three minutes' time to put on her oxfords. Time on the bus is waste time. So, if she puts them on there, that three minutes is saved. Three minutes a day is fifteen minutes a week, an hour a month, nine hours in a school year. The whole bus load will have it reported at school ten minutes after they've arrived. 'Hear the latest about Cress Delahanty? That crazy kid. She's figured out how to save nine hours a year—by putting on her shoes in the bus. What a girl! What a card!' "

Mrs. Delahanty's imitation of the high school crowd did not awaken her husband from his musing. "Nine hours," he murmured thoughtfully. "A whole work day. I suppose she can sleep that much longer?"

"John Delahanty," Mrs. Delahanty said, "you surely—" But in the midst of that she changed her tack. "Did you hear her phoning last night?"

"With one ear. I was busy at the time."

Yes, he had been. Mrs. Delahanty felt her lips pursing and unpursed them. Working on a three-sheet list: "Articles Needed for Complete Electrification of the Delahanty Ranch. Prices at Monkey Ward, Sears Roebuck, Martin and Dugdale."

"It would've paid you to listen."

Mr. Delahanty looked up from his Spanish rice. "Why?" he asked.

"She makes this call every night. Her algebra teacher made the sad mistake of saying in class that he couldn't possibly rest at night for wondering whether the class had done its homework. So Cress calls him."

"What does she say?"

"She says," Mrs. Delahanty said crisply, " 'This is Crescent Delahanty reporting, Mr. Holcomb. I have finished my homework. I hope you will sleep well now.' " About this exploit Mrs. Delahanty, feeling that such a lily needed no gilding, made no comment.

Mr. Delahanty appeared to choke a little on his Spanish rice. "More red pepper than usual in this today," he said.

Mrs. Delahanty said, "I have been making that dish for seventeen years and I put exactly the same amount of red pepper in it now as I did then."

"Maybe my mouth is getting more sensitive with the years."

"Maybe so," Mrs. Delahanty agreed. "But I doubt it."

"I suppose that really was carrying things a little far?"

Mrs. Delahanty waited for a more adequate summing up of the situation.

"I should think Mr. Holcomb would be over any night now to strangle her," Mr. Delahanty said.

This seemed quite a lot more likely to Mrs. Delahanty and she relaxed somewhat, pleased to find that the family still contained two sane members. Mr. Delahanty's sudden whoop of laughter, however, dispelled this happy supposition.

With that laugh still in her mind's ear, Mrs. Delahanty handed her husband the *Tenant Hi-Lights* at lunch a few days later. "Cress gave this to me this morning before she left for school," she said. "I think maybe she thought we would like some time alone to digest it." The paper was folded to the column called, "The Hi-Light's On ———," by I. Marcum. This week's Hi-Light was on "Cress Delahanty, That Crazy Freshman," and there was a drawing of her in the center of the column in her fur-topped bedroom slippers holding an oxford in each hand. "Read it out loud," Mrs. Delahanty said. "I want to be sure I wasn't seeing things when I read it."

After some preliminary smoothing and folding, which the *Hi-Lights* didn't need, Mr. Delahanty read in an expressionless voice, "Crazy or Cagy? Freshman girl sole discoverer of way never to be on her uppers, and you are a heel if you suggest that this is not the last word on this soulful subject. Personally, the ice blonde freshman can vamp us any time she wants to." Mr. Delahanty stopped reading. "Gertrude, do you really want me to go on with this?"

"Yes," Mrs. Delahanty said, "I do."

Mr. Delahanty took up the *Hi-Lights* again, but before continuing he said, "Ice blonde! Why, Cress is nothing but a mere child."

"A color is a color, I suppose," Mrs. Delahanty answered mildly, "regardless of age."

"Ice blonde is something more than a color," Mr. Delahanty argued, but when Mrs. Delahanty asked him to explain he could do no more than mention two or three movie stars.

"Go on reading," Mrs. Delahanty urged. "There's a good deal more."

Mr. Delahanty gave the *Hi-Lights* a couple more of the flattening whacks it did not require and continued. "Personally the ice blonde freshman can vamp us any time she wants to. We get a boot out of Delahanty. We pumped Cress and this is her version of what she calls 'Delahanty's Law,' or, to add our own interpretation, 'What You Do on the Bus Doesn't Count.'"

Mr. Delahanty paused once more and Mrs. Delahanty waited expectantly but about Delahanty's Law and its interpretation he had nothing to say.

"It goes on, Gertrude, as you doubtless remember, this way," he said. "No nit-wit she, Cress, and we quote, thus explained her discovery while we listened, tongue hanging

out, so to speak, and all unlaced with interest. 'I, in my
tireless search for efficiency, discovered that I spent fifteen
minutes a week putting on and tying my shoes. Now if I
did this on the bus, time ordinarily lost, as all bus riders
know, in useless chatter, I would gain one hour a month,
or one full working day a year.'

"Asked what she intended doing with this 'saved' time,
Cress answered demurely, 'Study.' Asked what, she re-
plied, 'Algebra. Mr. Holcomb, you know, can't rest nights
if the homework for his class isn't done.' (See next week's
Hi-Lights for the Holcomb-Delahanty story. Adv't.)
Asked what her ultimate goal was, Cress said, 'Oxford.'

"Excuse us please now while we pull on our own Con-
gressional Gaiters (not on a bus, thus losing, according to
Delahanty's Law, three minutes). We're going to hot-foot
it over to Cress's. Got a little equation we want help with.
Delahanty + I. Marcum = ? See next week's column for
answer (Adv't.)."

Mr. Delahanty folded the *Tenant Hi-Lights* into a
compact oblong and threw it toward the fireplace which
he missed. "What have we got for dessert?" he asked.

"It's right there before you," Mrs. Delahanty said, indi-
cating the raisin pie by his plate. Mr. Delahanty grunted
and began slowly to eat.

Mrs. Delahanty didn't feel like raisin pie herself.
"John," she asked, "what's your opinion of that?"

"My opinion is that I. Marcum will go far. We'll turn
on the radio any day now and hear I. Marcum's report on
the love life of Lana Turner."

"What do you really think, John?"

"I think it's a pity and a crying shame."

"You'll speak to Cress then?"

"It wouldn't do any good. What can we say to her? Stop saying and doing funny things?"

"Yes, we can."

"Sure, we can. But in the first place we can't stop her and in the second place if we could stop her, Cress would hate us for the rest of her life. I tell you, she's finding out who she is. At that age the only way to know whether craziness is your trademark is to *be* crazy. It's something you've got to do."

"I didn't have to."

"No, Gertrude, you didn't."

This quick admission hurt Mrs. Delahanty. She felt slighted, left out. She was no list-maker like John and Cress, but surely she had her share of craziness? They were not the two dark chaotic ones, were they, while she was no more than the dependable housewife of known and small dimensions?

"Once on a dare I wore a dress to school hindside foremost."

"Gertrude," Mr. Delahanty said, "you never had to bother trying on attitudes. You were born wearing one that fit beautifully."

Still, and startled, at this sudden turning of the conversation, Mrs. Delahanty watched her husband eat raisin pie. He paused to ask, "Don't you want to know its name?"

Mrs. Delahanty nodded, mutely.

"Radiant loving kindness."

This unexpected and extravagant compliment made Mrs. Delahanty feel shy. It was too extraordinary for her to deal with instantaneously and she put it aside for later consideration. "Whatever you think about Cress, John, I'm going to speak to her. I think it's my duty and I'm going to warn her at the first opportune minute."

The first opportune minute came that very afternoon and Cress, after being warned, went in tears to her room. She came out, ate her supper wordlessly, then went again to her room. When Mrs. Delahanty heard the lid of the bamboo desk creak down she said to her husband, "There is Cress writing out a list of reasons for hating me."

"What now?" Mr. Delahanty asked and Mrs. Delahanty with no heart for dish-washing said, "Come on in by the fire and I'll tell you."

Mr. Delahanty settled himself in the morris chair which had been his father's and Mrs. Delahanty stood in front of the fireplace, close to the fire until her calves began to scorch, then on the edge of the hearth until they cooled.

"This afternoon," she said, "Cress came skipping and hopping home from the bus clapping those two horrible bedroom slippers together over her head like castanets."

"Cymbals," said Mr. Delahanty.

"Together, anyway, and happy as a lark. It seems they had an assembly today—"

"Assemblies, assemblies," said Mr. Delahanty. "Bird

imitations, football rallies, talent shows. When do the kids go to school?"

"Assemblies," said Mrs. Delahanty, who went to P.T.A., "provide the children opportunity for participation in life situations."

"Is that thought to be a good thing? A life situation, if you ask me, is just about to engulf Cress. If you ask me a little participation in something un-life-like on the order of ancient history or the ablative case is what Cress has a crying need for. A little more life participation and she'll bust apart at the seams. I can hear them—"

"John," Mrs. Delahanty said, "I just want to tell you what Cress told me. And what I told her. I don't give a whit one way or another about assemblies. The point is, they had one. And when Mr. DuMont came out on the stage—"

"Who is this Mr. DuMont? A bird imitator?"

"Mr. DuMont is the vice-principal in charge of student activities. He has premature gray hair, a beautiful tan, and sings 'On the Road to Mandalay' so, Cress says, you can feel the waves rising and falling beneath you. He . . ."

"That's enough about DuMont," Mr. Delahanty said, "unless you've got some Mothersills handy."

"I've seen him," Mrs. Delahanty said, "and he really is nice. He has . . ."

"He came out on the stage . . . ," Mr. Delahanty reminded her.

"He came out onto the stage to give them what Cress

called a little pep talk about less lavatory art in the future, please."

"What?" said Mr. Delahanty in a strong voice.

"John, please try just to listen. I don't know why the school does what it does or why Cress calls things by the names she uses. All I want to do is tell you what happened."

"O.K.," Mr. Delahanty said, "I'm listening. Tell me."

He had the look of a man who has not yet had his say out but Mrs. Delahanty went on in spite of it. "On his way out Mr. DuMont stumbled over a pair of tennis shoes somebody had left on the stage. He stooped, picked them up by the strings, swung them back and forth, and then said in what Cress reports as being a perfectly dead-pan, side-splitting way: 'I see Delahanty has been here.' Like Kilroy has been here, you know."

"I know," Mr. Delahanty said.

"Then when everyone had stopped laughing at that, he said: 'They look like my size, but as a student of Delahanty's Law I intend to wait until I'm on a bus to try them on.'"

"Mr. DuMont's trademark appears to be craziness too," Mr. Delahanty remarked.

"The kids seem to love him."

"Why not?" asked Mr. Delahanty. "The kids are one with Mr. DuMont."

"I thought you approved of craziness. I thought that was what we've been arguing about."

"Gertrude, I haven't been arguing and what I approve

of is not craziness but freedom to find out who and what you are."

"Well, Cress thinks she's found out. She thinks she's a wit. Or a wag. Or the school jester. She says that about Delahanty's Law really panicked them and that not an eye in the auditorium but was on her. Even though she was sitting in an obscure spot under the balcony in the midst of one hundred and seventy-two other freshmen and practically invisible."

"She didn't say anything about standing up, or whistling and waving her handkerchief to help them see her, did she?"

"Now, John. Anyway when she finished, and I hated to do it because she was as happy as—"

"A prima donna?" suggested Mr. Delahanty.

"Oh no! A baby who's picked its first flower. Well, when she finished, I told her everything I've been thinking. I told her to stop it at once. That it was cheap and silly to play to the grandstand that way and that she was going to regret getting a reputation as a hare-brained clown when she was really a good, sweet, solid, sensible child." Mrs. Delahanty was unable to keep her voice from trembling.

"What did Cress say?"

"She said, 'Good, solid, sensible, sweet,' as if I had—as if I had reviled her. She said 'child' as if I had called her— a bastard. Then she began to cry."

Mr. Delahanty nodded and nodded as if this were all an old story to him.

"Then she stopped crying long enough to say that I didn't understand a thing. Not her. Not school. Not young people in general. Not Mr. DuMont. Not I. Marcum. And she said her constant prayer was that when she grew up and had children that she would not forget what it was like to be young. The way I have. And she said that for three months at school she *had* been sweet, solid, and sensible. And where had it gotten her? At the end of three months of that, she had been a complete nonentity and not a soul at school could've told you who Crescent Delahanty was. And now at the end of three weeks of planned living, with craziness for her trademark, she is a great success and she doubts there is even a custodian at school who has not heard of Crescent Delahanty and Delahanty's Law. 'In fact,' I said, 'you are now a character.' She said yes, she was, and proud of it. Then she went to her room. But before she left she said, 'Anyway my father understands me.' And now she is in there making a list headed, 'What's Wrong with Mother.' But I don't care. I had to tell her."

Mr. Delahanty caught at the edge of Mrs. Delahanty's skirt as she switched away from the fire and toward him, and pulled her down onto his lap. "Don't try to comfort me," she said, struggling to get up. "You think one way and I think another. That's all there is to it."

"I think just what you think, Gertrude—except that I think Cress will have to find it out for herself. She'll wake up pretty soon, and it'll be a painful awakening but it's bound to come."

Mrs. Delahanty, in spite of herself, was settling back and relaxing. "You believe that?"

"Of course. You don't think our daughter's a fool, do you?"

"No," Mrs. Delahanty said, letting her head, finally, rest at ease against her husband's shoulder. "No, how could I? Cress recapitulates you."

The "awakening," as Mr. Delahanty had named it, came the first week in December. The rains which had held off through the whole of November arrived the minute the November leaf on the calendar was torn off and made up by their abundance for their lateness. On Friday afternoon Mr. Delahanty, happily housebound by the downpour, sat before a drowsy fire working on his electrification lists.

On the other side of the fire Mrs. Delahanty was shelling English walnuts preparatory to sugaring them for annual Christmas gifts to eastern relatives. She listened to the pleasant blend of sounds, fire sighing, pen scratching, nut shells cracking, and behind and giving body to the blend the fine heavy sound of the constant rain. She was, she thought, reasonably happy. Then, as the pile of walnut kernels rose in the crock on the floor by her side, she decided that there is no such thing as reasonable happiness since happiness, like love, is without reason. A reasonable happiness is usually simply all the reasons one can think of for not being unhappy.

"I am not unhappy because my family is in good health

and I myself am well, and a good and needed rain is falling and we have a tight roof over our heads and the fire
is drawing beautifully." No, she thought, that is not
enough. Happiness, like love, fills the heart and does not
need to be accounted for. Joy washes away knowledge of
numbers. The one, two, threes. That was why, she supposed, John's lists had offended her. If you could analyze,
you were not in love. Or at least she was not. She was ana-
lyzing now. That was the reason she knew she was not
happy. And continuing to analyze she knew she would not
be until Cress was herself once again.

Cress came in from the bus, as Mrs. Delahanty recognized this fact; but she was neither the old Cress, solid and
sensible, nor the new one, crazy and show-off. This Cress
had been crying. She had on a hooded raincoat but she had
walked up from the bus with the hood hanging down her
shoulders and her hair, soaked to the scalp, was lank and
mousey. She was no ice blonde now. I. Marcum would
scarcely recognize her. Water dripped from her cheeks and
beaded her eyelashes and stood in the corners of her mouth
which she held with unchild-like firmness. She went without a word to the fireplace and stood there with her back
to her parents while occasional drops of water hissed off
her raincoat onto the andirons. Then she turned around
to face them, and it was the first time Mrs. Delahanty
had ever heard adult resignation in her daughter's voice,
adult acceptance of the fact that the source of one's joy is
also often the source of one's sorrow. I may have forgotten

what it's like to be a girl, she thought, but Cress is learning what it's like to be a parent.

"You have a perfect right to say I told you so now if you want to, Mother," Cress said. "You told me I was getting to be a character and I was, all right."

"What do you mean, Cress?" her father asked.

"I mean I'm Character," Cress said bleakly. "I'm 'Irresponsible Delahanty,' I'm that 'Crazy Kid.' If I said I was dying, people would laugh." Water ran out of her hair and across her face and dripped off her chin, but she scorned to wipe it away.

"I made a good speech to the Student Council and they laughed at every word I said. They laughed and held their sides and rolled in their chairs like loons."

"What speech was this, Cress?"

"The speech everybody who is a candidate for an office has to make to them. Then if they like you, they nominate you. I was a candidate for freshman editor. What they nominated me for was *Josh* editor. Josh editor. A two-year-old can be Josh editor. All you need to be Josh editor is a pair of scissors to cut out jokes with. I wouldn't be Josh editor if they shot me for not being. It's a silly job."

"Take off your coat, Cress," Mrs. Delahanty said, and Cress, not ceasing to speak, began also to unbutton. "I would've been a good editor and I told them the reasons —like I was responsible, knew the meaning of time, would see that the assignments were in on time and so forth. They laughed like hyenas," she said, not bitterly, but reflectively. "They said, 'This is the richest thing yet. Delahanty is a real character.' So they nominated me for Josh editor and I'm branded for life."

She threw her raincoat, which she had finished unbuttoning, onto the floor, said, "I have ruined my life," and walked out of the room, no longer trying to hide the fact that she was crying.

Mr. and Mrs. Delahanty still held the positions they had had when Cress entered; Mr. Delahanty, pen above his list; Mrs. Delahanty nutcracker in one hand, cracked unshelled nut in the other. Mr. Delahanty said, "I guess you were right. I guess it would've been better to have forbidden it."

"I did forbid it," Mrs. Delahanty said, "in so far as I could, and you can see what came of that." Mechanically she picked the kernel from the nut she still held, then got up and threw the pan of shells into the fire. Mr. Delahanty had gone back to his list-making and she felt almost the first wave of dislike she had ever known for her husband. That was really carrying objectiveness a little too far. Electrification at a time like this. She herself was going to Cress. She looked coldly down at Mr. Delahanty's list as she passed and saw what had been, and was, in the process of being written there. "Spit. Spit. Spit Delahanty. Big Spit Delahanty. Spit. Spit."

John saw her look and let her take his hand. "I told you it was a dark time," he said quietly.

"John—you still remember? It still matters?"

All he said was, "You go on in to Cress. She's your youngest baby."

She let go his hand and went toward Cress's room. She didn't know what she would or could say when she got there. Maybe, "Cress, people like you and your father have to try on more than one way of being and doing to see who you are. And you're bound to make mistakes." Maybe she would say, "My sweet sensible daughter." But she would surely hug her and kiss her. Her arms, as she heard through the closed door those catching sobs, already felt that stocky body grow quiet. She opened the door and said, "Cress, honey."

Winter II

It was the last Thursday in January, about nine in the evening, cold and raining. The three Delahantys sat close about the living-room fireplace—Mr. Delahanty at the built-in desk working on his schedule, Mrs. Delahanty on the sofa reading, and between them, crosswise in the wing chair, their daughter.

Cress was apparently studying the program of the folk-dance festival in which she was to appear the next evening. For the most part, however, she did not even see the program. She saw, instead, herself, infinitely graceful, moving through the figures of the dance that had been so difficult for her to master.

The high school folk-dancing class was made up of two kinds of performers—those with natural ability, who had themselves elected the class, and those who, in the language of the physical education department, were "remedials." The remedials had been sent into the class willy-nilly in an effort to counteract in them defects ranging from antisocial attitudes to what Miss Ingols, the gym teacher, called "a general lack of grace." Cress had achieved the class under this final classification but now,

108

at midterm, had so far outgrown it as to be the only remedial with a part in the festival.

The first five numbers on the program, "Tsiganotchka," "Ladies' Whim," "Meitschi Putz Di," "Hiawatha," and "Little Man in a Fix," Cress ignored. It was not only that she was not in these but that they were in no way as beautiful as "Road to the Isles," in which Mary Lou Hawkins, Chrystal O'Conor, Zelma Mayberry, Bernadine Deevers, and Crescent Delahanty took part. The mere sight of her name beside that of Bernadine Deevers, Tenant High School's most gifted dancer—most gifted *person*, really—instantly called up to Cress a vision of herself featly footing it in laced kirtle and starched skirts, a vision of herself dancing not only the outward steps of "Road to the Isles" but its inner meaning: what Miss Ingols had called "the achievement of the impossible."

Cress thought that she was particularly adapted to dancing that meaning because she had so recently come that way herself. If she had been given three wishes when school opened in September, two of them would have been that Bernadine be her friend and that she herself succeed in the folk-dancing class. Both had then seemed equally impossible. Now not only did she have a part in the festival but Bernadine was her dear friend and coming to spend the week end with her. At the minute the evening reached what she considered its peak of mellowness, she intended to speak to her father and mother about the festival and Bernadine's visit. She was exceedingly uncertain about their performances on both these occasions.

The rain suddenly began to fall harder. Cress's father, hearing it on the roof, watched with gratification as the water streamed across the dark windowpanes. "Just what the oranges have been a-thirsting for," he said.

Mrs. Delahanty closed her book. "How's the schedule coming?" she asked her husband.

"O.K., I guess," said Mr. Delahanty.

Cress looked up from the festival program with embarrassment. The schedule was one of the things she wanted to speak to her father about. She hoped he wouldn't mention it while Bernadine was visiting them. Every winter, as work on the ranch slackened, he drew up a schedule for the better ordering of his life. And every spring, as work picked up, he abandoned it as easily as if it had never been. Last winter, he had made a plan called "A Schedule of Exercises to Ensure Absolute Fitness," which included not only the schedule of exercises and the hours at which he proposed to practice them but a list of the weaknesses they were to counteract. He had even gone so far, last winter, as to put on a pair of peculiar short pants and run six times around the orchard without stopping, arms flailing, chest pumping—a very embarrassing sight, and one that Cress could not possibly have explained to Bernadine.

This winter, the subject of her father's schedule-making was not in itself so unsuitable. He had bought a new encyclopedia set and was mapping out a reading program that would enable him, by a wise use of his spare time, to cover the entire field of human knowledge in a year. The name of the schedule, written at the top of a sheet of

Cress's yellow graph paper, was, in fact, "Human Knowledge in a Year." There was nothing about this plan that would call for embarrassing public action, like running around the orchard in shorts, but it was so incredibly naive and dreamy that Cress hoped her father would not speak of it. Bernadine was far too sophisticated for schedules.

"Where are you now on your schedule, John?" Mrs. Delahanty asked.

Mr. Delahanty, who liked to talk about his plans almost as much as he liked to make them, put down his pen and picked up the sheet of paper on which he had been writing. "I've got all the subjects I want to read up about listed, and the times I'll have free *for* reading listed. Nothing left to do now but decide what's the best time for what. For instance, if you were me, Gertrude, would you spend the fifteen minutes before breakfast on art? Or on archaeology, say?"

"You don't ever have fifteen minutes before breakfast," Mrs. Delahanty said.

Mr. Delahanty picked up his pen. "I thought you wanted to discuss this."

"Oh, I do!" said Mrs. Delahanty. "Well, if *I* had fifteen minutes before breakfast, *I'd* read about archaeology."

"Why?" asked Mr. Delahanty.

"It's more orderly that way," Mrs. Delahanty said.

"Orderly?" asked Mr. Delahanty.

"A-r-c," Mrs. Delahanty spelled, "comes before a-r-t."

Mr. Delahanty made an impatient sound. "I'm not going at this alphabetically, Gertrude. Cut and dried. What I'm thinking about is what would make the most interesting morning reading. The most interesting and inspiring."

"Art is supposed to be more inspiring," Mrs. Delahanty told him. "If that's what you're after."

This seemed to decide Mr. Delahanty. "No, I think science should be the morning subject," he said, and wrote something at the top of a sheet—"Science," Cress supposed. "That's better," he said. "That leaves art for the evening, when I'll have time to read aloud to you."

"Don't change your schedule around for my sake, John," said Mrs. Delahanty, who hated being read to about anything.

"I'm not. All personal considerations aside, that's a more logical arrangement. Now the question is, which art?"

This seemed to Cress the moment for which she had been waiting. "Dancing is one of the earliest and most important of the arts," she said quickly.

"Oho!" said her father. "I thought you were in a coma."

"I've been rehearsing," said Cress.

"Rehearsing!" exclaimed Mr. Delahanty.

"In my mind," Cress said.

"So that's what was going on—'Ladies' Whim,' 'Tsiganotchka'—"

"Father," Cress interrupted, "I've told you and told you the t's silent. Why don't you take the program and practice the names? I'll help you." Cress got up and took the program across to her father.

"Practice them," said Mr. Delahanty with surprise, reading through the dances listed. "What do I care how they're pronounced? 'Korbushka,' 'Kohanotchka,'" he said, mispronouncing wildly. "I'm not going to Russia."

"But you're going to the folk-dance festival," Cress reminded him.

"I don't *have* to go. If you don't want—"

"I do, Father. You know I want you to go. Only I don't want you to mispronounce the names."

"Look, Cress," Mr. Delahanty said. "I promise you I'll keep my mouth shut the whole time I'm there. No one will know you have a father who can't pronounce. Mute I'll come and mute I'll go."

"I don't want you to be mute," Cress protested. "And even if I did, you couldn't very well be mute the whole time Bernadine's here. And Bernadine's the star of the program."

"To Bernadine," said Mr. Delahanty, referring to the program once again, "I shall speak of 'Badger,' and 'The Lumberman's Two Step.' I can pronounce them fine and they ought to hold Bernadine. She's not going to be here long, is she?"

"Friday to Monday," said Mrs. Delahanty.

"In that case," said Mr. Delahanty, "maybe I should find another one. How about 'The Irish Jollity,' Cress? Do I say that all right?"

"Now, John!" Mrs. Delahanty reproved her husband.

"It's all right for him to joke about it to me, Mother.

But he mustn't before Bernadine. Bernadine's serious about dancing. She's going to be a great artist."

"A great dancer?" Mrs. Delahanty asked.

"She hasn't decided what kind of an artist yet," Cress said. "Only to be great in something."

"Well, well," said Mr. Delahanty. "I'm beginning to look forward to meeting Bernadine."

"You already have," Cress told him. "Bernadine was one of the girls who rode with us to the basketball game."

Mr. Delahanty squinted his eyes, as if trying to peer backward to the Friday two weeks before when he had provided Cress and four of her friends with transportation to an out-of-town game. He shook his head. "Can't recall any Bernadine," he said.

"She was the one in the front seat with us," Cress reminded him.

"That girl!" exclaimed Mr. Delahanty, remembering. "But her name wasn't Bernadine, was it?"

"No," Cress told him. "That's what I wanted to explain to you, because tomorrow's Friday, too."

Mr. Delahanty left desk and schedule and walked over in front of the fireplace. From this position, he could get a direct view of his daughter.

"What's this you're saying, Cress?" he asked. "Her name isn't Bernadine because tomorrow's Friday. Is that what you said?"

"Yes, it is," Cress told him, seriously. "Only it's not just tomorrow. Her name isn't Bernadine on any Friday."

Mr. Delahanty appealed to his wife. "Do you hear what I hear, Gertrude?"

"Mother," Cress protested, "this isn't anything funny. In fact, it's a complete tragedy."

"Well, Cress dear," her mother said reasonably, "I haven't said a word. And your father's just trying to get things straight."

"He's trying to be funny about a tragedy," Cress insisted obstinately.

"Now, Cress," Mr. Delahanty urged, "you're jumping to conclusions. Though I admit I think it's queer to have a name on Fridays you don't have the rest of the week. And I don't see anything tragic about it."

"That's what I'm trying to tell you, only you keep acting as if it's a joke."

"What is Bernadine's name on Fridays, Cress?" asked her mother.

"Nedra," said Cress solemnly.

Mr. Delahanty snapped his fingers. "Yes, sir," he said, "that's it! That's what they called her, all right."

"Of course," said Cress. "Everyone does on Fridays, out of respect for her sorrow."

"Just what *is* Bernadine's sorrow, Cress?" her mother asked.

"Bernadine never did say—out and out, that is. Once in a while she tries to. But she just can't. It overwhelms her. But we all know what, generally speaking, must have happened."

"What?" asked Mr. Delahanty. "Generally speaking?"

Cress looked at her father suspiciously, but his face was all sympathetic concern.

"On some Friday in the past," she said, "Nedra had to say no to someone. Someone she loved."

"How old is Berna—Nedra?" Mrs. Delahanty asked.

"Sixteen," Cress said. "Almost."

"Well, it couldn't have been too long ago then, could it?" her mother suggested.

"Was this person," Mr. Delahanty ventured, "this person Nedra said no to, a male?"

"Of course," said Cress. "I told you it was a complete tragedy, didn't I? His name was Ned. That much we know."

"Then the Nedra is in honor of—Ned?" asked her mother.

"In honor and loving memory," Cress told her. "On the very next Friday, Ned died."

Mr. Delahanty said nothing. Mrs. Delahanty said, "Poor boy!"

"I think he was probably more than a boy," Cress said. "He owned two drugstores."

After the elder Delahantys had thought about this for a while, Mr. Delahanty asked, "This 'no' Bernadine—Nedra—said, was it to a proposal of marriage?"

"We don't ever ask about that," Cress told her father disapprovingly. "It doesn't seem like good taste to us."

"No, I don't suppose it is," Mr. Delahanty admitted.

"Anyway," Cress said, "that's Bernadine's tragedy and we all respect it and her wish to be called Nedra on Fridays. And tomorrow is a Friday, and it would be pretty awful to have her upset before the festival."

Mr. Delahanty stepped briskly back to his desk. "Don't you worry for a second, Cress," he said. "As far as I'm concerned, the girl's name is Nedra."

"Thank you, Father," Cress said. "I knew you'd understand. Now I'd better go to bed." At the door to the hallway, she turned and spoke once again. "If I were you, Father, I wouldn't say anything about your schedule to Bernadine."

"I hadn't planned on talking to her about it. But what's wrong with it?" Mr. Delahanty sounded a little testy.

"Oh, nothing," Cress assured him. "I think it's dear and sweet of you to make schedules. Only," she explained, "it's so idealistic."

After Cress left the room, Mr. Delahanty said, "What the hell's wrong with being idealistic?"

Cress thought that her friend, in her costume for "Fado Blanquita," the Spanish dance in which she performed the solo part, looked like the queen of grace and beauty. And she said so.

"This does rather suit my type," Bernadine admitted. She was leaning out from the opened casement window of Cress's room into the shimmering, rain-washed air. She tautened her costume's already tight bodice, fluffed up its already bouffant skirt, and extended her hands in one of the appealing gestures of the dance toward the trees of the orange orchard upon which the window opened.

"Is your father a shy man?" she asked.

Mr. Delahanty, who had been working near the drive-way to the house when the two girls got off the school bus an hour before, had, instead of lingering to greet them, quickly disappeared behind a row of trees. Now, in rubber boots, carrying a light spade that he was using to test the depth to which the night before's rain had penetrated the soil, he came briefly into sight, waved his spade, and once again disappeared.

"No," said Cress, who thought her father rather bold, if anything. "He's just busy. After the rain, you know."

"Rain, sunshine. Sunshine, rain," Bernadine said understandingly. She moved her hands about in the placid afternoon air as if scooping up samples. "Farming is an awfully elemental life, I expect. My father"—Bernadine's father, J. M. Deevers, was vice-president of the Tenant First National Bank—"probably doesn't know one element from another. I expect your father's rather an elemental type, too, isn't he? Fundamentally, I mean?"

"I don't know, Nedra," Cress said humbly.

"He's black-haired," Bernadine said. "It's been my experience that black-haired men are very elemental." She brought her expressive hands slowly down to her curving red satin bodice. "You must have a good deal of confidence in your family to let them go tonight," she went on briskly.

"Let them!" Cress repeated, amazed at the word.

"Perhaps they're different from my family. Mine al-

ways keep me on pins and needles about what they're going to say and do next."

"Mine, too," Cress admitted, though loyalty to her
father and mother would not permit her to say how greatly
they worried her. She never went anyplace with them that
she was not filled with a tremulous concern lest they do or
say something that would discredit them all. She stayed
with them. She attempted to guide them. She hearkened to
every word said to them, so that she could prompt them
with the right answers. But *let* them! "They always just
take it for granted that where I go, they go," she said.
"There's not much question of letting."

"Mine used to be that way," Bernadine confided. "But
after what happened at the festival last year, I put my
foot down. 'This year,' I told them, 'you're not going.' "

"What happened last year?" asked Cress, who had not
then been a dancer.

"After the program was over last year, Miss Ingols
asked for parent participation in the dancing. And my
father participated. He danced the 'Hopak,' and pretty
soon he was lifting Miss Ingols off the floor at every other
jump."

"Oh, Nedra," Cress said. "How terrible! What did
Ingols do?"

"Nothing," said Bernadine. "That was the disgusting
part. As a matter of fact, she seemed to enjoy it. But you
can imagine how I suffered."

Cress nodded. She could. She was thinking how she
would suffer if her father, in addition to mispronouncing

all the dances, went out on the gymnasium floor and, before all her friends, misdanced them.

"Are your parents the participating type?" Bernadine
asked.

Cress nodded with sad conviction. "Father is. And
Mother is if encouraged."

"You'd better warn them right away," Bernadine said.
"Your father just came in the back door. You could warn
him now."

Cress walked slowly down the hallway toward the
kitchen. Before the evening was over, her father, too,
would probably be jouncing Miss Ingols around, and even
calling Bernadine Bernadine—then all would be ruined
completely, all she had looked forward to for so long.
In the kitchen, she noted signs of the special supper her
mother was cooking because of Bernadine: the cole-slaw
salad had shreds of green peppers and red apples mixed
through it tonight to make it festive; the party sherbet
glasses, with their long, icicle stems, awaited the lemon
pudding. But her mother was out of the kitchen—on the
back porch telling her father to hurry, because they would
have to have dinner early if they were to get to the festival
in time.

"Festival!" Cress heard her father say. "I wish I'd
never heard of that festival. How did Cress ever come to
get mixed up in this dancing business, anyway?" he asked.
"She's no dancer. Why, the poor kid can hardly get
through a room without knocking something over. Let
alone dance!"

"That's *why* she's mixed up with it," her mother explained. "To overcome her awkwardness. And she *is* better."

"But is she good enough?" asked her father. "I'd hate to think of her making a spectacle of herself—to say nothing of having to sit and watch it."

"Now, John," Cress heard her mother say soothingly. "You're always too concerned about Cress. Will she do this right? Will she do that right? Stop worrying. Cress'll probably be fine."

"Maybe fall on her ear, too," her father said morosely. "They oughtn't to put so much responsibility on kids. Performing in public. Doesn't it worry you any?"

"Certainly it worries me. But all parents worry. And remember, we'll have the star of the performance with us. You can concentrate on Nedra if watching Cress is too much for you."

"That Nedra! The only dance I can imagine that girl doing is one in which she would carry somebody's head on a platter."

Cress had started back down the hall before her father finished this sentence, but she had not gone so far as to miss its final word. She stopped in the bathroom to have a drink of water and to see how she looked in the mirror over the washbasin. She looked different. For the first time in her life, she saw herself through other eyes than her own. Through her parents' eyes. Did parents worry about the figures their *children* cut? Were they embarrassed for *them*, and did they wonder if they were behaving suitably,

stylishly, well? Cress felt a vacant, hollow space beneath
her heart, which another glass of water did nothing to
fill. Why, *I'm* all right, Cress thought. *I* know how to
behave. I'll get by. *They're* the ones . . . but she looked
at her face again and it was wavering, doubtful—not the
triumphant face she had imagined, smiling in sureness as
she danced the come-and-go figures of "Road to the Isles."

She went back to her room full of thought. Bernadine
was changing her costume, and her muffled voice came
from under all her skirts. "Did you tell them?" this
muffled voice asked.

"No," said Cress, "I didn't."

"Why not? Won't you be worried?"

"They're the ones who are worrying. About me."

"About you?"

"Father thinks I may fall on my ear."

Bernadine, clear of her skirts, nodded in smiling agreement. "It's a possibility that sometimes occurs to *me*, Cress
dear."

Cress gazed at her friend speculatively. "They're worried about you, too," she said.

"Me?" asked Bernadine, her smile fading.

"Father said the only dance he could imagine you doing
was one with a head on a platter."

"Salome!" Bernadine exclaimed with pleasure. "Your
father's imaginative, isn't he? Sympathetically imaginative?"

"I guess so," Cress said, and in her confusion told everything. "He keeps schedules."

"Schedules?"

"For the better ordering of his life."

Bernadine laughed again. "How precious!" she said.

Then, as if remembering after too long a lapse the day and her bereavement, she said, "Neddy was like that, too."

"Neddy," repeated Cress, pain for the present making Bernadine's past seem not only past but silly. "Oh, shut up about Neddy, *Bernadine!*"

Bernadine gave a little gasp. "Have you forgotten it's Friday?"

"I don't care what day it is," Cress said. She walked over to her bed, picked up the pillow, and lay down. Then she put the pillow over her face.

Winter III

They were both in the side yard when Cress got home, her mother cutting zinnias, her father holding them and complaining about the coming wind. Cress heard him as she rounded the house. Looking at her over the top of his armload of flowers he called out, "I suppose you ordered this weather, Cress?"

This was an old pleasantry and Cress didn't bother to reply to it. Instead she asked, "Is it all right if I start taking music lessons on Monday?"

"Music lessons!" her father echoed, as if she had suggested lessons in tight-rope walking or sword-swallowing. "At your time of life?"

Cress had been urged toward music lessons since the age of six. Neither her father nor mother could carry a tune and both of them felt that if Cress would express only a little inclination toward music, their stock would have, culturally, made some advance. But no. Cress would have none of it. Sit on a piano stool hour after hour going tink, tink, tink, with the ends of her fingers, when she could be using all of her body swimming? Or climbing hills? What a crazy idea! How could people waste their lives that

124

way? Now she had to overcome their disbelief in her seriousness.

"I never *heard* music until recently," she told them. "I had no idea what music was, *really.*"

Her mother paused in her zinnia-cutting. She held one big saffron-colored flower, the size of a salad plate, and ran her thumb around its cog-wheel edge. "Does Mrs. Charlesbois play?"

"Yes. She does. She plays beautifully. She's a former pupil of Levinsky."

"Where would you take lessons?" her mother asked. "At school?"

"No," Cress said. "From Mrs. Charlesbois. She's going to give lessons. There's an announcement in this evening's *Star.*"

Mr. Delahanty handed Cress his zinnias and walked over to the edge of the front lawn. He picked up the *Star,* unrolled it and turned to the back page.

"It's not with the want ads," Cress told him proudly. "It's on the society page."

Mr. Delahanty turned back to the society page, searched a second, then read aloud: "Mrs. Luther Charlesbois announces the formation of classes for instruction in the art of piano-playing, beginning on September 17th. Mrs. Charlesbois, a former pupil of Levinsky, is recently of Los Angeles where she made frequent appearances on the concert stage. She has been guest soloist with such well-known organizations as the Southern California Orpheus Club and the Los Angeles Lyric Society, and is a valued and distinguished addition to Tenant music circles. Mrs. Charlesbois is prepared to accept both beginning and advanced pupils. To contact her phone 153."

Mr. Delahanty re-rolled his paper and took a swing at a low flying swallow. "I wondered how long it would be before she'd have to take a hand at supporting that rundown ranch. One job in the family wouldn't turn the trick."

"It's probably more the loneliness than anything else," Mrs. Delahanty said, handing Cress the saffron zinnia. "Up there on the edge of the hills with nothing but coyotes and buzzards for company a good deal of the time."

Mr. Charlesbois worked in the city, a job on the Los Angeles *Times* of some kind, no one seemed to know just what. Certainly not a reporter, for he was the exact opposite of a news-hawk in appearance, being dumpy (this in spite of the fact that he was not short), with a round, worried face. The Charlesboises had no car and Mr. Charlesbois cut across the Delahanty ranch each morning on his way to catch the 7:10 Pacific Electric, and again each evening, on the evenings when he came home, after getting off the 6:20. So the Delahantys had had plenty of opportunities to appraise his looks.

"Why didn't Charlesbois ask somebody who knew something about ranching before buying that place?" Mr. Delahanty asked, as if Mrs. Delahanty had never mentioned loneliness. "All right," he said, "why didn't he ask me?"

"It was cheap," Mrs. Delahanty said. "Maybe cheapness was an item."

"Cheapness of that kind is always dear in the long run."

The Charlesbois ranch had been planted in the late '20's when orange prices were so high that all land in Tenant which was not straight up and down and to which at least a little water could be piped had been cleared and planted. Now the shallow foothill soil, together with a decade of insufficient fertilizing and spraying had resulted in a grove, yellow-leaved, and overproducing, as dying stock will.

"Maybe it was more to get out of the city, than get a producing grove?" Mrs. Delahanty suggested.

Cress, uninterested in why the Charlesboises had located in Tenant, said again, "Is it all right if I start taking lessons Monday?"

She had first met Mrs. Charlesbois two weeks ago in the hills back of the Charlesbois ranch. She often went up there at sundown, for the pleasure of the run and for the wonderful, sad, alone-in-the-world feeling it gave her to look out over the darkening valley at that hour. She had been standing on Lookout Rock, half-childishly frightened by the cicadas buzzing about her heels with their rattlesnake sound, when a voice behind her said, "Don't jump please. I'm just another human being."

She *had* jumped, of course, and Mrs. Charlesbois had put out a steadying hand. "Couldn't you tell by the way the katydids stopped singing that someone was coming?"

"I didn't notice that they did stop."

"What! Not a Campfire Girl, not a Girl Scout?"

"I was a Blue Bird once," Cress had admitted, painfully bound to literal truth-telling, though she saw how unimportant it was.

"I would never have guessed it. You look far more like a quail or meadow lark. Even," she had added, laughing, "a road-runner."

Mrs. Charlesbois had looked like what? She had had on white shorts that first afternoon and a white blouse; but Cress had never seen her in shorts again and certainly never thought of her that way. She always wore white, though, white dresses that to Cress's mind were old-fashioned. They reminded her of dresses she had seen in her mother's snapshot albums, dresses with puffier sleeves and fuller skirts than women wore nowadays; and they were always made of materials, the names of which Cress had never before heard. It had become a kind of game with them. Cress would rub a fold of the full skirt between thumb and forefinger and ask, "Is this marquisette?", the day-before's dress having been of marquisette, and Mrs. Charlesbois would reply, "No silly, *this* is poplin." Or, "Soisette," or "Madras shirting." They were all wash materials anyway, and they were always freshly washed and ironed and had that sweet smell garments sun dried and newly ironed have. Though that was far from being Mrs. Charlesbois' only scent: she used perfume and lots of it—

Quelques Fleurs, which was perfect for her. How terrible
if she had been attracted to—though with her taste she
couldn't have been, of course—something unsuitable like
My Sin or *Shocking.* No, *Quelques Fleurs* with its fra-
grance, almost, of ripening fruit as well as of flowers, *was*
Mrs. Charlesbois. It was almost as if the manufacturers
had been thinking of her when they made it. Cress tried
to catch, through the rank, really weedy, smell of the
massed zinnias she held, a trace of *Quelques Fleurs* from
the inside of her own elbow where Mrs. Charlesbois had
sprayed some.

"Neither yes, no, nor kiss my foot," her father was saying, "let alone thank you?"

"What?" Cress asked, though as she said the word, a
recording-machine, deep inside her head, played back the
sentences she had not heard. "Sure. Start lessons Monday
if you want to. Why not?"

"Thank you," Cress said, hearing that re-playing.
"Thank you more than I can say."

Her father looked at her meditatively, seemed about
to speak, then without speaking, unrolled, once again, his
paper. Her mother, clipping off dead blossoms, said, "I
declare I can *smell* that Santa Ana, coming."

Cress, chin-deep in the zinnias, stood looking out toward
the gap between Old Saddle Back and Old Gray Back,
the gap the wind blew through. A little smudge about
the size of a man's thumb was lodged there. Already,

sixty miles away, the wind was blowing. It would still be
blowing on Monday when she started her lessons. That
made Monday seem less far away.

Anybody, Cress thought happily, who takes music lessons is crazy, crazy, crazy. Music lessons were fully as awful as she had imagined and the worse the better, for they
proved that there was nothing she wouldn't do to be near
Mrs. Charlesbois. It was the afternoon of her fourth lesson and she was having the half-hour of supervised practice which followed it. Mrs. Charlesbois was in the kitchen,
clinking and stirring, busy with the special supper she was
cooking; but now and then, with her starched skirts rustling
like palm leaves, she swept into the living room, put a wet,
or floury, hand over Cress's hand, separated her fingers,
straightened her wrist and said, "Thumb under third
finger, under, under, under. Make it smooth, not fast.
Smooth, smooth. That is the way." Then she would rustle
back to the Beef Stroganoff, leaving the air about the piano
sweet with *Quelques Fleurs*.

Thumb under third finger smoothly was hard work.
Cress labored with it. There was no light, quick tink, tink,
tink, when she practiced—as once she had imagined there
would be, but a slow heavy tunk. Tunk. Tunk.

"You are the worst of my pupils," Mrs. Charlesbois
would declare, fondness in her voice. "I have never seen
your like."

"Worse than Linton Matthews?" Cress would ask.
Linton was a boy her own age, taking piano lessons to
help his stammering.

"No comparison at all."

"Worse than Don Rivers?" Don Rivers was a grown man, though a young one, a road superintendent who was taking, of all things, lessons on the accordion. "Am I worse than Don Rivers?" The worse she was, Cress thought, the more it proved that Mrs. Charlesbois was her friend as well as her teacher. Perhaps more friend than teacher.

"Beside you, Crescent Delahanty," Mrs. Charlesbois had said, "Don Rivers is a great artist, a second Liszt."

Cress had laughed at this exaggeration. Mr. Rivers left his accordion, an enormous thing, almost as large as a bale of hay, at the Charlesboises' between lessons. The tent at the road camp where he lived with the other men who were working on the Imperial Highway Project was not a safe place to keep so expensive an instrument.

"When does he practice?" Cress had asked.

"Here, after lessons. Like you."

"But I practice at home, too."

"Mr. Rivers isn't a beginner like you. He doesn't really need practice. All he needs is a place to play where people understand a taste for music—and don't make fun of a grown man who loves it—the way they do down at the road camp."

"In the movies," Cress had said, "men on jobs love music. They always sit around campfires at night singing and playing. Railroad gangs and cowboys and miners. And the like."

"Not the kind of music Mr. Rivers plays and understands. Not serious music."

"Maybe not," Cress had admitted. She really didn't know, and she liked Mr. Rivers. He had his lesson just after hers. Five to six. Her lesson was late because of school, and his, because of his work, was still later. After dinner would've been even better for him, Mrs. Charlesbois said, but it was too much to expect Mr. Charlesbois to put up with the eternal sound of music. "He has to hear enough as it is, just listening to me, without the additional uproar of pupil-practice being added."

"Uproar," Cress had echoed, hating Mr. Charlesbois for thinking of his wife's playing as an uproar. "I think he's terrible. He must loathe music, really."

But Mrs. Charlesbois would not hear a word against her husband, ever. "Now, Cress," she had warned, then softened her warning by saying, "You know very well Cress, that the accordion is not everyone's instrument."

Maybe not. Anyway, Cress liked Mr. Rivers. He had driven her home one night when her lesson had run late and he had arrived early. He was a dark, beak-nosed young man, smiling, but not very talkative and as polite to her as he was to Mrs. Charlesbois. He was going to have dinner tonight with her and Mr. and Mrs. Charlesbois. Cress would have preferred to have been the only guest, but she knew quite well that Mrs. Charlesbois couldn't show preference for any one pupil.

At seven o'clock Mrs. Charlesbois took Mr. Charlesbois' plate off the table. He was obviously not coming home on the 6:20 and there wasn't another car out from the

city until 9:47. "He hates being pinned down to any particular hour," Mrs. Charlesbois explained. "And actually
he can't always tell. Things come up." She lit the candles
in the branched crystal holders, brought in the iced fruit
cups and the three of them sat down at the round table.
Cress couldn't keep her eyes off Mrs. Charlesbois. She
had on one of her usual white wash dresses, though this
one was cut low enough in the neck to show the first firm
upswelling of her bosom. The skin there, like that of her
face, was a rosy-olive and, somehow, velvety-looking.
She had three little scarlet pom-pom dahlias just in front
of her knot of chestnut hair; they were so solid looking you
could almost imagine them to be wooden, the carved heads
of the skewer-like pins it would take to hold up hair so
long and so heavy. Mrs. Charlesbois presided as if the
dinner were very important; yet she was so laughing and
girlish, her round brown arms passing food with all the
grace of piano playing, that Cress felt, beside her, quite
heavy and matronly.

Sometimes she felt sorry for Mr. Rivers, Mrs. Charlesbois left him so much out of the conversation; as if he were
only an audience for her and Cress's talk. She would touch
Cress when she got up to change course, give her shoulder
a little squeeze or smooth one of her eyebrows with a delicate forefinger. She was almost incandescent, Cress
thought, burning bright, like Blake's tiger, her hands
flickering out to warmly touch, like flame-tips.

After dinner they sat in the living room. Mrs. Charlesbois brought the candles from the dining-room table and

put them on the piano. Then she lit two big chunky candles on the mantel and put a match to the already laid fire. Because there was greasewood in it, the smell was of outdoors, and this was strange in a living room with a grand piano and a bust of Beethoven on a white pedestal.

Mrs. Charlesbois stood, after the fire caught, looking at the room. "We have a festival of lights," she said in a low excited voice. "Oh do look how they glitter."

Cress did look and it was true. There were only two small rugs on the floor, and the bare floorboards reflected all the wavering unsteady lights. There were no curtains at the windows and though there were blinds, these were not pulled and the black night pressed against the glass like a depth of unfathomable water and bore the candlelight on the surface of its darkness as it were a mirroring pond or lake.

After they had looked for a while Mr. Rivers said, "Won't you please play for us?"

"No, not tonight," Mrs. Charlesbois said. "With you two, music is my business. Let's not have any business tonight. Let's visit, let's be friends. Let's have a festival of talk. You start, Cress."

Cress asked a question she had been wanting to ask for a long time. "Tell us about that picture," she said. "Please."

The picture, a large one in a narrow gilt frame, hung on the wall just above the keyboard of the piano so that Cress, when she practiced, often looked at it. The picture was of Mrs. Charlesbois as a girl. She wore a purple (the picture was hand-tinted) velvet dress, with a train, and there was white fur, ermine, Cress believed, around the neck and the edges of the great bell-shaped sleeves. On her head—she wore her hair long even then—was a golden tiara, just large enough to encircle the mound of her up-piled hair. "Was that," Cress asked, "the dress for your coming-out party?"

"Coming-out party! Oh, Cress!" Mrs. Charlesbois' laugh was like her hair and skin, warm, a mingling of rosiness and darkness. Her voice laughed at the funniness of that suggestion, but it cried, too, at something sorrowful in it. She left the fireplace and took the picture off the wall and holding it in both hands peered down into it as if it were a mirror. "Coming-out party! Sweet little Cressy. What would I have come out of? Or to?"

She carried the picture over to Mr. Rivers and Cress was the audience now as Mrs. Charlesbois, one hand on the back of Mr. Rivers' chair, addressed her talk to him.

"Were you ever in Oilinda?" she asked. "A little oil town up in the stubble hills, the houses throbbing all night with the pumps and the coyotes coming down at dawn to steal the kids' pet rabbits?"

Mr. Rivers looked up from the picture, saying no by a shake of his head.

"You've missed nothing," Mrs. Charlesbois declared. "I was born there. I think maybe I'm the only baby who ever was. Most pregnant women couldn't stand the smell of the oil and the constant throb of the pumps and the buzzards and snakes. Anyway I was born there and went to school there and was elected Queen of the County Fair there.

And that is the picture of me, Queen of the Orange County Fair."

"They couldn't possibly have elected anyone else."

"They could have, but they didn't. Fifteen or twenty other girls were candidates, but I won easily. Oil men make big money, or did then—and they are easy spenders. You voted," she explained, "by buying tickets at a quarter each. One man, a driller, bought an even hundred. So I won. I reigned for the five days of the Fair, rode around the county sitting on the back of a convertible and accompanied by a five-piece band. Such crazy nonsense! On the second night of the Fair, I was formally inaugurated, floodlights, a full band then, and so forth. They gave me this ring, that night. It was my prize for winning the election."

She held up her left hand and showed them the diamond she wore above her wedding ring. "It is small," she said, defending it against any belittling, "but deep and true in color." Then, looking over Mr. Rivers' shoulder, and speaking objectively, "She was really quite a pretty girl then."

There was a small silence, before Mr. Rivers, as if the truth must be spoken, however awkward or difficult, said, "She was *beautiful*, Inez. She still is."

It was the first time Cress had ever heard Mrs. Charlesbois called by her first name. She looked at her as if, beneath the familiar outline, she might see emerging a new and more intimate personage. And for a minute that hidden person did partially emerge; that sweet, regal, newly crowned girl was there in the room, more real than the grown-up music teacher.

"Oh, Mr. Rivers," she said. "Thanks, thanks. I was seventeen then and that was seventeen years ago. Why, I'm old enough to be Cress's mother. Easily old enough."

At first, Cress thought proudly that Mrs. Charlesbois was saying, "Since I'm old enough, why don't I have a daughter like Cress?" But she wasn't sure, because the next words she said were, "Me, me, Inez Dresden."

She took the picture from Mr. Rivers and went to the window with it, and gazed into the picture, rather than at it, since that was the darkest spot in the room. "I was the first Queen they had ever had who could do anything except pose in a bathing suit or ride on a rolled-back convertible top. When they found I could play the piano, they had me play every night in the intermission between band pieces."

Cress said, "Oh, I wish I could have seen you. And heard you."

"I was just about as good then as I am now, I'm afraid."

"Afraid?" Cress said.

"One should grow, develop."

"Geniuses," Cress said fiercely, "*can't* improve like other people, can they? They start too near the top. There isn't room." Once again Cress had the feeling that the young queen was there in the room. But Mrs. Charlesbois, the music teacher, came back and chided her.

"Don't be silly, Cress." Nevertheless she ran her finger

over the glass of the picture, as if hunting for that lost fur and velvet. And diadem. "I met Luther the last night of the Fair," she said.

"Luther?" Cress repeated.

"Mr. Charlesbois. He came up onto the grandstand and played a duet with me. He'd had about one bottle of beer too much and someone had dared him to do it. We played Beethoven's *Appassionata* together."

Mr. Rivers, who knew about serious music, said, "The *Appassionata!*"

Cress said, "I didn't know Mr. Charlesbois played. I didn't know he even liked music."

"I don't think he does any more," Mrs. Charlesbois replied, taking the picture back to its place on the wall beside the piano.

Cress spent that night at the Charlesboises'. At ten thirty Mrs. Charlesbois asked, "Is there really any sense in your going home at this hour, Cress? Why don't I just call your mother and tell her you're spending the night here? There's no telling whether or not Mr. Charlesbois will be home tonight and while I'm not exactly afraid to stay alone here, I'm not exactly happy about it either."

Mrs. Delahanty of course said, "Stay," and after that Cress was often at the Charlesboises'. She would fall asleep in her room upstairs in the Swiss chalet, listening to the sound of Mr. Rivers' serious music on the accordion. She understood better now why Mr. Rivers' music was never going to keep men at a road camp sitting around a camp-

fire in the evening. She herself would have preferred the
Beer Barrel Polka to the mournful, uncadenced cries
which seeped upward to her. On the nights when Mr.
Charlesbois came home there was, out of deference to his
having grown away from music, no accordion-playing of
any kind, either serious or pleasant to hear.

Though Cress still felt considerable hardness of heart
toward Mr. Charlesbois for what appeared to her to be
his neglect of his wife and for his loss of interest in her
music, this feeling was tempered some by a talk she had
with Mr. Charlesbois himself. She had come home one
Saturday afternoon at the beginning of December on the
same Pacific Electric car as Mr. Charlesbois. She had spent
the night before with her grandfather in Whittier and
Mr. Charlesbois, through work early because it was Saturday, had taken the 4:10 out from town instead of the 6:20.
Cress hadn't seen him on the car and was surprised when
he alighted with her at the Tenant station.

They walked the mile to the Delahanty ranch together,
talking as they went. Cress saw that, though Mr. Charlesbois was neither handsome nor commanding, she had been
mistaken to think him nothing. His face *was* biscuit-
shaped, round, rather doughy and biscuit-colored, too.
And when he took off his hat, she could see, through his
thinning, dun-colored hair, the faint pinkness of his scalp.
But his eyes were a strong, flashing gray and when he
looked at her she was aware of his thoughtfulness; aware
that, as he talked, he thought of *her*. Mr. Charlesbois
seemed not only to leave himself behind but—could it be?

—to surround her with some kind of understanding and even sympathy as he talked. Would he do that? He, an elderly (Mr. Charlesbois was at least forty-five) almost bald man? But it was not a certain thing, of course. And in any case, she didn't mind.

When they reached the arroyo on the Delahanty ranch where their paths separated, Mr. Charlesbois stayed on for a few minutes talking. It was by now a clear, green winter evening. The rains were late and there was a summer warmness and dryness in the air. And though the scent of the Valencias, blossoming all about them, was typical of December, still their sweetness in the December evening belied winter. Mr. Charlesbois put his hat back on his head, but to one side, and with his baldness thus covered and with his cocky inquisitive stance, feet apart and head tilted downward toward her, Cress saw, as she never had before, how this man could be the one who had volunteered to play duets with the soloist at the County Fair.

"I hear you've been kind enough to keep Inez company on some of the evenings when I've been away."

"Yes," Cress answered, "I have. But it wasn't kindness." She was caught between a desire for very strong words and a desire not to be silly or sentimental. "It was a high privilege." This, because it sounded like a speech from her high school principal, she amended by saying, "I dearly love Mrs. Charlesbois." Though she would have told this to no one else; Mr. Charlesbois made her feel like being honest.

Mr. Charlesbois received this statement quietly. "I

know," he said. "Me, too. For seventeen years." Then, as
if he too feared the mawkishness Cress had tried to avoid,
he swept his hat off once again and made her a stiff, stocky
bow, "Us two great lovers," he said.

They both laughed at this: Cress at the idea of a man
of Mr. Charlesbois' age being called a lover of any kind,
let alone a great lover. The tension that the word *love* had
set up being relieved by the laughing, Cress said, "I'm
staying this Monday night too." Then, because a little
embarrassment still lingered, she said self-consciously, "If
you're home I can play my first real piece for you."

"What is it?" Mr. Charlesbois asked.

" 'Barcarole' from *The Tales of Hoffmann!* Simplified,
of course," she admitted.

"Well," Mr. Charlesbois said, "that's real progress."
He whistled a few bars, then sang, " 'Night in June, O
beauteous night.' And here it is December! June in December and night coming on. No, I won't be home Monday, but you can play it for me some other time. And you
take good care of Inez. It has always made her uneasy,
being alone."

Monday night was the most beautiful night she had had,
so far, at the Charlesboises'; and even though Mr. Rivers
stayed for dinner too she had come not to mind him very
much. In fact, once or twice when she and Mrs. Charlesbois had been alone for dinner some of the magic had been
missing. The outward surfaces had been the same; the
warm glowing skin, the fresh white dress, the usual kind

graciousness; but Inez Dresden, the young queen, had
been absent. And nothing Cress could say, no funniness or
compliment could bring her back; and once having seen
that Mrs. Charlesbois, no one was going to be content with
any other.

Also the presence of Mr. Rivers seemed to reconcile
Mrs. Charlesbois (and Cress had become reconciled to the
fact that Mrs. Charlesbois needed such reconciliation) to
the idea that she was old enough to be Cress's mother.
Cress had even heard her say once to Mr. Rivers, when
Cress had been out on the porch with the saucer of milk
for the cat, "Where has that child of ours disappeared
to?"

This was the first night they had had music after dinner.
"Inez," Mr. Rivers said (Mr. Rivers and Mrs. Charlesbois, now that they knew each other better, were always
"Don" and "Inez" to each other), "won't you play for us
this evening?"

Mrs. Charlesbois, who had always before said no to this
question, said, as if she had only been waiting to be asked,
"Of course, Don, I'll play for you. Then you can play for
me and Cress can play for both of us." And that was what
they did, no questions asked about, "What do you want,"
or any nonsense of that kind. Mrs. Charlesbois went to the
piano and began to play as if, long ago, it had been settled
that whatever Mr. Rivers wanted, she wanted too.

Cress had no idea what was being played; and she saw
clearly enough that this was no time—though she had a
bent that way—for picking up musical facts, memorizing

the names of composers and compositions. The sounds which Mrs. Charlesbois' strong pink-nailed fingers brought out from the piano were to be heard and felt, not labeled or pigeonholed. Now, Cress thought, Mrs. Charlesbois is not the young queen, but something greater, even. But what was greater than a young queen? Summer was greater, Cress thought, and a deep river and the ocean, and it was of these she was reminded. Mrs. Charlesbois was *so* beautiful! She had a kind of satiny sheen like plums or grapes, fully ripe but not yet touched. It was a winter's night but Mrs. Charlesbois put summer in the room. June in December, as Mr. Charlesbois had said. The scent of her perfume was as warm and gusty as if it came off a real garden where real flowers opened their trumpets to invite the sun's entry down to the last granule of golden pollen.

Mr. Rivers' playing was quite different, no summer sounds or scents came from that great instrument of his. What he played was night and storm and darkness, things anyone sitting in the dark would want music to blot out. Islands of sound! Silence between the islands. No way for a non-swimmer to get from one island to the next. Island after island, each new, and stranger than the last. The accordion, Cress supposed, was the nearest there was to a human lung, most able to cry and bewail and entreat. Stop, stop, she wanted to say to Mr. Rivers.

And he did stop, suddenly, with no sign given beforehand that a stop was coming, no flourish of any kind. No crescendo, Cress thought, using her newly acquired knowledge. Just cessation. His arms hung at his sides; that big external lung still hung from his neck. Mrs. Charlesbois did not say a word to him—any more than he had spoken to her when *she* finished playing. But she helped him out of the harness of that crying instrument, before turning to Cress.

"Now it's your turn," she said.

Up to the minute of that command Cress had supposed that she would play, that she was waiting to play. But when the command came she was suddenly tired and sleepy. And she saw how absolutely crazy the notes of her simplified "Barcarole" would fall into a room still echoing with those other notes. "If you'll excuse me," she said, "I think I'll go to bed."

She went to sleep at once and awakened to the sound of Mrs. Charlesbois and Mr. Rivers playing together. The music, much hushed by the time it reached the second story of the chalet, might have been dreamed. Cress rested on her elbow for a time listening, assuring herself by continuing to hear it, that it had not been. Listening, a line, then two lines of a verse she would like to write for Mrs. Charlesbois came to her mind. There was an empty place in her heart, which she would have to *do* something to fill. If she had been able to play her music, that might've taken away the pain of something unexpressed, undone. She turned on the light by her bed and got, from her school bag, paper and pencil. After she had put down the two lines, a third came by itself; but the fourth she could not get even by making lists of rhyming words. But no sooner had she turned out the light and tried to sleep than there it was. She made a fair copy of her verse and above it wrote, "A Few Lines for Mrs. Charlesbois." She was pleased by this title, by her modesty and understatement in calling what was actually her entire heart and devotion, "A Few Lines." Looking at her verse she had a sudden impatience with waiting for morning to give them to Mrs. Charlesbois. The emptiness of the act unperformed wasn't filled simply by writing. And though she couldn't awaken Mrs. Charlesbois at that hour of the night to say, "Here is a poem, Mrs. Charlesbois, to say how much I love you," she could slide her sheet of paper under Mrs. Charlesbois' door where she would find it the moment she opened her eyes in the morning. Cress went down the stairs barefooted, filled with the happiness of doing.

Either Mr. Charlesbois hadn't come home at all on Tuesday and Wednesday nights, or he had come home on the late car. Cress had kept a sharp look-out for him but hadn't seen him. On Thursday night she walked into the Tenant station and was waiting in the shadow of the building when the 6:20 pulled in. She watched Mr. Charlesbois come heavily down the steps, noted that he was hatless and that he had pushed his newspaper, folded any old way, into his bulging coat pocket.

"Mr. Charlesbois," she called, "Mr. Charlesbois."

At first, all of her sorrow and pity had been for herself. She remembered hearing Mrs. Charlesbois telling everybody, one time when she had gone into town with her and her mother, "Oh Cress is *more* than a pupil. She stays with me almost every Monday night." "Yes, Mr. Charlesbois *is* away a good deal, but Cress stays with me when he's gone." "Oh no, I'm not lonely. I almost look forward to the nights Luther is gone, Cress and I have such good times."

And I was nothing to her, Cress thought bleakly. Nothing. She perhaps even loathed me, but she had to put up with me, I was so convenient for her. After a while she had stopped thinking of her own hurt and deception and thought of Mr. Charlesbois. What of him? He was still deceived. He still believed. "Us two great lovers." And we were nothing to her. Nothing. Me, a convenience, and Mr. Charlesbois, a hindrance.

She ran out of the shadow calling in a louder voice, for Mr. Charlesbois, head down, was already walking away from the station. He turned at her call and came back toward her. "Why, Cress!" he exclaimed. "I didn't see you on the car. You been up visiting your grandpa again?"

"I wasn't on the car," Cress said. "I came especially to meet you."

Mr. Charlesbois looked at her with some surprise, but said only, "That was nice of you." They started their homeward walk in silence. It was a dark moonless night with only a handful of stars to be seen between the big threatening clouds. Except that the path they traveled was well known to both, going would have been difficult.

As it was, they walked quickly, sometimes abreast, sometimes single file. Cress, who had believed that her sense of duty was strong enough to make it easy for her to tell Mr. Charlesbois what she had to tell him, could find no words with which to begin.

Mr. Charlesbois himself said, "Well, did you play your 'Barcarole' Monday night? Simplified version?"

"No," Cress answered. After a while, she said, "They played, though."

"They? You mean Inez and Mr. Rivers?"

"Inez and Don," Cress said.

"Inez and Don. That's right. First names don't come easy to me. It's a wonder I'm not calling you Miss Delahanty."

Cress went on desperately, in spite of this playfulness. "I came down to meet you, Mr. Charlesbois, to tell you that Monday night—"

Mr. Charlesbois finished for her. "To tell me you had a fine shindig Monday night. Played music. Made fudge, maybe."

"No," Cress said, "oh no, it was nothing like that. It was the opposite of that. I came to tell you that afterwards, after I went to bed I came downstairs and—"

"And left Inez a poem," Mr. Charlesbois said. "I have it right here." He clapped a hand against his coat pocket. "I like it. I've thought what you say in it a lot of times myself, but I haven't your gift for words. I can say it by heart, if you want me to."

"Don't," Cress cried. "Don't say it. You wouldn't want to say it if you knew—"

"Knew," Mr. Charlesbois interrupted her. "Why I know everything, Cress. By my time of life there's nothing a man doesn't know—whether he wants to or not. All a man at my time of life can learn is new ways of saying things like this pretty rhyme of yours:

> *She had the dark and windswept beauty*
> *Of the hills from whence she came.*"

"No," Cress insisted. "No, please don't say it." She made one more effort. "You and I, Mr. Charlesbois, we both—"

He once again completed her sentence for her. "We both love Inez."

"Did," Cress said. "We did."

"No," Mr. Charlesbois contradicted her, "we do. I know everything, and you know quite a lot. For a girl your age—," he said, and though it was too dark to see, his voice sounded as if his face might have that same crooked Jack O'Lantern smile she had seen when he said, "Us two great lovers"—"for a girl your age you're downright loaded with knowledge. And both of us love Inez. Only you can say it in rhyme and I can't. So long," he said. "It's late and it's going to rain before I get home if I don't hurry." From some distance up the arroyo he called back, "I'm still looking forward to hearing you play that 'Barcarole.' Grown-up version, no simplifications. I might even play it with you sometime."

Cress stopped beside a lemon tree near the house for a while before going in. The light shone outward onto the waxy yellow fruit and she picked a lemon, rolled it between her hands until it was soft, then broke its skin with her thumbnail and began to suck it. A few drops from the coming storm spattered onto her forehead and hands. She wanted to stay out in the rain, be drenched, muddied, cold. She knew exactly what she had tried to do and why. It was perfectly clear to her and now she would like to stay out until she was half-drowned and worried about, then go in and be made the center of a considerable to-do, dried and warmed and comforted. She went in just as she was, however, scarcely dampened, pausing at the door only long enough to throw away her half-sucked lemon.

Spring I

It was early spring. In the arroyo, a quarter of a mile south of the Delahanty ranch, cactus was already blooming. Meadow larks sang their liquid, worldly songs. Butcher birds, rich in insects, impaled their surplus stock on suitable thorns. Road-runners ran for pleasure and without pursuit. Ground squirrels, bereft of what little caution they possessed at other seasons, frisked at great distances from their burrows. Buzzards floated low, their shadows dark on the grass which the sun, almost down, was gilding. But the air was still warm, the day still lovely, and the arroyo continued to echo, as it had for the past hour, with the stateliest measures ever molded by the lips of man—the long rolling periods of Virgil.

"Ancora de prora iacitur, stant litore puppes," Edwin concluded, taking his eyes from his invisible audience and looking inquiringly at Cress, who sat across the ravine from him on a large, sun-warmed boulder.

"Begin at the beginning and say it all over again," Cress urged. "Not that I don't think you're perfect right now," she added frankly.

Edwin relaxed somewhat, but still looked worried.

"Perfect means incapable of improvement," he reminded Cress.

"Well, *I* don't see how you can improve it," Cress protested, her fair, freckled face flushed with sunlight and her pleasure in Edwin. "You know every word by heart and you pronounce every word right. What more *could* you do?"

Edwin scowled across the narrow arroyo as if its smallness hampered his imagination. "If I was good enough," he said slowly, "I could put the whole spirit of Virgil in it." He paused and looked earnestly at Cress. "If I was good enough, I could put the whole spirit of the ancient world in it."

"Well, O.K., then," Cress said enthusiastically. "Let's do that. Let's be absolutely terrific."

Edwin replied a little stiffly, "I wasn't joking."

"Me either," Cress exclaimed, surprised. "Wasn't that what you meant, Edwin?"

"I wasn't thinking about being terrific or anything like that."

Cress, who had been, said, "I'm sorry, Edwin."

"You kind of always overstate things, Cress."

"Edwin," Cress asked leaning forward, "do you think I'm impetuous?"

Edwin removed his steel-rimmed spectacles and cleaned them on an oblong of white canton flannel neatly feather-stitched in blue around the edges. Cress took note of it, thinking she might make Edwin another for his birthday if she could learn to feather-stitch in three months' time, which she doubted.

"Do you, Edwin?" she repeated.

Edwin resettled his spectacles. "I think you're pretty hasty sometimes, Cress."

Hasty was not the same as impetuous, and Cress returned to Virgil. "Go on, Edwin," she said. "Say your part through from the beginning again."

"It's your turn to say your part," Edwin told her.

"My little two lines," Cress scoffed.

"A chain is no stronger than its weakest link," Edwin said honestly, "and your lines have their place in the play."

The play, "Scenes from *The Aeneid*," was to be presented in one week's time by the Latin department of Tenant High School. Each spring, wearing togas and huaraches, garlanded with chaplets of eucalyptus leaves and carrying short swords carved from Sunkist orange boxes, the Latin classes demonstrated to assembled parents their mastery of the language. This year's demonstration was unusually ambitious and Edwin as narrator was, after Aeneas himself, its most important male personage.

Looking at Edwin now Cress thought that, with his dark hair falling in a jagged line across his high white forehead and his eyes lifted to the rim of the arroyo, he looked like a great tragic actor, or perhaps, except for his glasses, Hamlet himself. It was easy to imagine that the battlements of Elsinore had been of the same smoky gray-green as the tall cactus which now served him as a back-

drop and that the problems which he pondered had to
do, not with a high school Latin play, but with love and
death and guilt and madness.

"Edwin," she asked, "would you like to play Hamlet?"

Edwin shook his head. He had no illusions about his
qualifications as an actor, nor about the problem he had
presented to Miss Freitag, Latin teacher and director of
the play. He was the best student in Miss Freitag's classes
and he could memorize Latin verse more easily and de-
liver it with greater sonority and conviction than any
other of her pupils. But his appearance was woefully un-
classic and he knew it. And not only did he have a non-
Virgilian look, but in some unfortunate manner he com-
municated a non-Virgilian look to all which, until he came
upon the scene, appeared authentic.

Edwin seemed to be a touchstone of reality. The minute he stepped onto the stage, chaplets, which, until that
time had been easily recognizable as of the true laurel,
became nothing more than circles of wire incompletely
covered with eucalyptus leaves. And the short swords, for
all their aluminum paint, immediately reverted to the soft
pine of orange boxes. Worst of all the toga, which on the
other boys was a picturesque and dignified garment, obviously appropriate for poets and statesmen, appeared on
Edwin to be a costume downright unsuitable for public
wear.

Miss Freitag had tried putting Edwin into a short tunic,
but that had been even worse. Atlas Peake, the Aeneas
of the play, took one look at him, thus scantily covered,

and said, "You're sure lucky to be living today, Skinny. The Romans would've exposed you at birth."

Miss Freitag, while considering this statement untactful, thought it probably true, and was proud of her final solution of the problem posed by Edwin. She developed the part of narrator for him, kept him off the stage entirely and clothed him in a manner intended to suggest a professor of the classics: thin legs hidden by striped gray professorial trousers, narrow shoulders encased in a frock coat, necessary spectacles given the appearance of scholarship by a length of dangling black grosgrain ribbon. These make-shifts, which Edwin saw truly enough as occasioned by his deficiencies, appeared to Cress to be nothing more than a tribute to his uniqueness. Ignoring his reluctance to talk about himself as an actor she said again, "I bet you could play Hamlet if you wanted to."

"Well, I don't want to," Edwin answered shortly.

"O.K.," Cress persisted stubbornly. "You don't have to, but you could. Go on," she said hurriedly before Edwin had a chance to contradict her, "say your part through once again. I can say mine on the way home."

Edwin straightened himself as if about to begin, then lowered his chin and looked about. The arroyo while narrow, was deep, a sandy, golden, cactus-filled waste, lonely, strange, and, at this time of the day, a little mysterious.

"This probably looks a good deal like Africa," he said.

"Africa?" Cress asked, her thoughts far from there.

"Where Aeneas met Dido."

"Oh! It's a good place to be practicing then, isn't it?"

Edwin nodded. "It's funny, isn't it, Cress? Here we are reciting Virgil, and Virgil didn't even know the New World existed. Let alone the United States."

"Let alone California."

"Let alone this arroyo and you and me in it," Edwin said, and he and Cress both laughed.

"Maybe he does know," Cress said. "Maybe he's alive some place and listening."

"Do you believe in life after death, Cress?" Edwin asked seriously.

Cress sighed with pleasure. Perhaps they would now have a philosophical discussion. That was one of the things she liked so much about Edwin; he was interested in everything and would talk about everything: life, death, honor, immortality, transubstantiation. Did everyone see the same chair? If you could hear the intervals of silence in music, would they be music, too? At what minute did a bird swallowed by a cat cease to want to chirp and begin to want to meow, instead?

Now she replied judiciously, "Yes, I do, Edwin. Don't you?"

Edwin didn't reply. Far off in the Santa Ana valley Cress heard a train whistle. A hummingbird dropped into the arroyo, whirred disappointedly about the wild tobacco blossoms which were still too green for honey. A lizard ran halfway up the boulder she sat on, looked at her, then ran down again. "Don't you, Edwin?" she asked again.

But Edwin only shook his head. Evidently he was not in the mood for a philosophical discussion this afternoon.

"You got time to hear me through once more?" he asked.

"Of course," Cress said. "That's what I've been waiting for. Begin at the beginning. Begin at, 'Arms, I sing, and the man.'" Cress imitated somewhat Edwin's polished, declamatory style. But without the Latin words the imitation was rather flat.

"Arma virumque cano Troiae qui primus ab oris," Edwin began, his r's liquid as water, his vowels like trumpet notes. Cress settled back comfortably on her boulder to listen. If Edwin didn't look like a Roman, he at least came nearer than anyone else in Tenant to sounding like one. He had gotten as far as Dido's curse, "Et iam prima novo spargebat lumine terras," when glancing at the bank above Cress's head he broke off.

"Hi, there!" he said in a flat voice.

Cress turned about. There, above her, was Clarence Rambo. He was known, because of his red hair and ability to cover ground, as the Crimson Rambler. The Crimson Rambler now stood, legs wide apart and hands in pockets, regarding her and Edwin curiously.

"The Rambler himself," Cress said without enthusiasm. She and Clarence were not on good terms. He had passed her a note in study hall which she, after seeing the first few words, had taken up to the wastepaper basket and ostentatiously torn into a thousand pieces without further reading. Now, as Clarence dropped down into the arroyo, Cress looked with renewed distaste at his red, good-natured face and his small reddish-brown eyes.

"Nice hide-out you two got here," he observed.

"Hide-out!" Cress exclaimed.

"Yeh, hide-out. What you two do down here, anyway?"

"Do? We're practicing," Cress told him with dignity.

This struck the Rambler as being very funny and he laughed immoderately. "Practicing!" he was finally able to say. "What you two practicing down here in your hide-out, Cress?"

"We're rehearsing for the Latin play," Edwin said. He pulled his copy of "Scenes from *The Aeneid*" from his pocket as if to prove it. " 'Scenes from *The Aeneid*,' " he explained.

This also seemed very funny to the Rambler. He laughed so hard that the skin was drawn tightly across the two bony protrusions above his eyes and the eyes themselves were narrowed to the merest slits.

" 'Scenes from *The Aeneid*'! Say, did you ever hear this?" he asked them.

> *"Latin is a language,*
> *Least it used to be,*
> *First it killed the Romans,*
> *Now it's killing me."*

"We've heard it," Cress said. "It's very, very funny. Also very, very old."

"I know some more," Clarence said. "New. Want to hear some more? Also in Latin."

"Beat it, Rambo," Edwin said. "Get out of here. We're busy."

The Rambler looked at Edwin very coolly. "Drop dead, Skinny," he advised, "and save the doctor's bill." Then he turned again to Cress. "You want to hear some more, Cress? I can make up poetry. Latin poetry."

"You and Virgil," Cress said lamely.

"Sure, me and Virgil. I sing of arms and the woman."

"Shut up, Rambo," Edwin said.

"I'm not talking to you, Skinny. You go off some place and practice. Practice acting alive. This poem's about you, Cress. Amo, amas, amat, Delahanty's plenty hot. How d'you like that, Cress? More truth than poetry, huh?"

Edwin threw "Scenes from *The Aeneid*" to the ground. "Cut that out, Rambo."

"Oh hell, Skinny," Clarence said easily, "don't let it worry you just because it didn't come out of a book. You'd be surprised what ain't in books. Besides that's just the beginning. Amo, amas, amat, Delahanty's . . ."

Clarence stopped suddenly and Cress, who had been watching him, too amazed and shocked to speak, turned toward Edwin. Edwin was holding threateningly aloft a large and very spiny section of the cactus plant beside which he stood.

"Don't that hurt, Skinny?" Clarence asked finally, a little uncertainly.

"You shut up," Edwin told him, "or you'll soon find out."

"Why, Skinny," Clarence said, "don't you know that's just like pulling a gun on an unarmed man?"

"O.K.," Edwin said. "I've got a gun and you're un-

.armed. And you better shut up and get out of here or I'll fire it. And another one right behind it." Edwin extended his free hand in the direction of the cactus plant at his side.

"Two-gun Skinny!" Clarence's voice was heavy with sarcasm.

"Three-gun, four-gun, if you don't beat it," Edwin said, unmoved.

"I was only making a little joke. Cress don't . . ."

"Shut up about Cress," Edwin told him, lifting the cactus section menacingly, "and beat it."

"You don't have to keep saying it," Clarence said. "I got no desire to hang around where I'm not wanted. Where all people can think of to do is to bop each other over the head with pieces of cactus." He climbed the embankment slowly and unconcernedly. At the top he turned around. "Any time you get brave enough to meet me without a gun, Skinny, just let me know. Things'll be different then."

Whistling loudly to show his indifference to the entire affair, Clarence disappeared. When he could no longer be heard Edwin dropped the cactus, walked over to the boulder which Cress had vacated and sat down. He leaned forward, shoulders hunched, looking at the ground.

"Does your hand hurt, Edwin?" Cress asked.

The hand with which he had held the piece of cactus was red, full of spines and already swelling, but Edwin shook his head.

"I guess you're pretty ashamed of me," he said in a low voice.

"Ashamed!" Cress exclaimed.

"Pulling a gun on an unarmed man that way. I guess that was pretty tricky, all right. And cowardly."

"Cowardly," Cress repeated vehemently. "Why, he'd have beaten you to nothing, Edwin, if you hadn't. And said anything he wanted to about me."

"A brave man would've fought him on even terms," Edwin said dejectedly. "Knuckles to knuckles."

"Knuckles to knuckles!" Cress cried in disgust. "Why, you did fight him on even terms. He's got muscles and you've got brains. You fought his muscles with your brains."

"I've got some muscles," Edwin said.

"Of course you have. But Clarence Rambo's got ten times more muscles than anybody I know. It would be like David's throwing away his sling-shot and going out to wrestle with Goliath. It would be stupid. Knuckles to knuckles," she said again scornfully.

"Is that the way it seems to you, Cress?"

"Yes, it is. And besides, it didn't hurt David any to use his sling-shot and it must have hurt you terribly to pick up that cactus. In fact, it was the most courageous thing I ever saw. Or heard of."

Cress hurriedly lifted Edwin's hand and began to examine it. "I can pull out these big ones now," she told him, "but I can't do anything about the little ones without tweezers."

When most of the large needles were out Edwin said, "You never did get to say your part, Cress."

"I don't care," Cress told him. "Anyway, I think *The Aeneid* is silly, really."

"Silly!" Edwin sounded shocked.

"The men are all right, I guess. But Dido! Building herself a funeral pyre because Aeneas was sailing away from her."

Edwin was silent while Cress worked on a final needle. Then he said, "Dido *loved* Aeneas."

"Well, of course," Cress answered. "But building herself a funeral pyre because he was leaving her!"

"What would you have done, Cress?"

"*I* would have built myself a boat and sailed right after him."

Edwin said nothing. "Which would *you* want a woman to do, Edwin?" Cress asked.

"I don't think anyone's going to jump on a funeral pyre for me or sail after me in a boat, either one," Edwin said.

Cress finished her work on Edwin's hand before she spoke again. "Of course, in this day and age that's just figuratively speaking. Funeral pyres and sailing away in boats and so forth."

Edwin stood up and with his good hand pushed back his hair which had fallen further than usual over his forehead.

"Figuratively speaking," he said, "I wouldn't like *you* jumping on any funeral pyres, Cress." He examined the remaining cactus needles closely for a second or two, then looked up. "That is, if I were sailing away—which I wouldn't be."

Cress's heart gave a sudden deep throb, so that there

seemed to be no room left in her chest for lungs or breathing. She walked over to where "Scenes from *The Aeneid*" lay, picked it up and returned it to Edwin.

The sun, just setting, filled the arroyo with a flood of gold and crimson and the meadow larks, as if aware that day was ending, sang with a kind of sad sobriety. Cress, able to breathe easily again, looked about. It's a thousand times more beautiful here than Africa ever was, she thought and started to say so. But remembering what Edwin had said about overstatements, she contented herself with, "I bet Africa's not half this beautiful, Edwin."

Spring II

"Who is this Ina?" her mother asked Cress. "Where does she live? And I thought Honor Gallagher was your friend of the moment?"

"Honor is," Cress said, "but she can't be thinking of me every minute. And Ina's full name is Ina Inez Wallenius," Cress answered. Cress didn't care whether her mother said yes or no about this visit. Without telling her mother, she had assigned to her for the moment the role of Fate, and Cress was perfectly willing that Fate should know everything she knew about Ina, and then decide.

"If her initials had been I.W.W. instead of I.I.W., she would have stood for International Workers of the World," Cress said as an afterthought.

"It's Industrial Workers of the World, isn't it?" said Mrs. Delahanty.

"Anyway, it's wobblies," Cress said.

"Wobblies!" exclaimed Mrs. Delahanty. "Your friend Ina isn't a wobbly, is she?"

"As a matter of fact, she isn't even a friend," said Cress.

"Not a friend?" said Mrs. Delahanty, puzzled. "I

thought you just said she was. I thought that was why you wanted to visit her."

"What I should have said," Cress told her mother, "was that Ina wants me to be her friend."

Cress didn't think it would be good taste to say just how much Ina seemed to want her for a friend, or of any use to try to explain to her mother the high school's complicated social structure—a structure upon whose upper level she was now located, but not established, and upon whose lower level Ina stood, reaching upward. A visit could put Ina up where she was, or just as easily put Cress down where Ina was. Cress thought it was her duty to give Ina her chance. This was one of the reasons she preferred to leave everything to Fate. There was more responsibility in the visit than she cared to assume.

"She's a nice girl, is she—this Ina?" Mrs. Delahanty asked.

"Oh, she's a very nice girl!" Cress said. She didn't say that in her opinion Ina was too nice. She didn't know how that could be possible, but some people were certainly too nice. Ina wasn't too nice in the sharp, old-maidish way to which some girls are born—handkerchiefs in clean triangles, salt for their hard-boiled eggs in little waxed-paper envelopes, hair ribbons in ready-tied bows. These girls, whatever their ages, seemed like aunts to Cress and she got on very well with them all.

Ina hadn't been born too nice; she was that way because she chose to be. And one nice habit she had was just about the most unpleasant Cress had ever heard of. She carried a toothbrush to school with her and every day after lunch she brushed her teeth in the girls' rest room. And when she had finished, she would smile at herself, so that at least half her teeth, softly shining, were reflected in the basement's gloomy mirror. Then she would slowly close her full, pink lips over her clean teeth. Why did that seem a bad thing to do? Cress couldn't say, but it did, and, watching her, Cress would shudder.

"Wallenius," said Mrs. Delahanty. "What is that? Swedish?"

"I guess so," Cress said. "Anyway, Ina looks it."

Ina's hair was yellow white and she wore it in heavy, sausage-like curls low on her neck. She had heavy white eyelashes and eyebrows, big, murky blue eyes, and a loose-appearing golden skin.

"She's an orphan," Cress said, thinking she should perhaps give Fate more to work on.

"An orphan," her mother repeated. "She surely doesn't live alone, does she?"

"I mean she's a half orphan," said Cress, for whom a mother was still the most of a family. "Her father's alive. Ina keeps house for him."

"Have you ever seen him?" Mrs. Delahanty asked.

"No, but he's a good old man, I know," Cress said with assurance. "Ina says he reads a chapter from the Bible out loud before every meal."

"Well," said Mrs. Delahanty, "I don't know a reason in the world why you shouldn't stay all night with Ina if you want to. Where does she live?"

"Kettle Hill," said Cress.

"Oh!" said her mother.

Cress knew what that "Oh!" meant. Kettle Hill, although only ten miles distant by road and six by the spur line down which the tank cars rumbled, carrying the hill's oil to the main tracks, seemed a world away from the valley, with its orange groves, where the Delahantys lived. It was off by itself, separated by its location and work from the ranches. Did anyone ever go there, Cress wondered, besides the drillers, the riggers, the pumpers, and their families? One evening when out for a drive, Mr. Delahanty had taken his family up the road to Kettle Hill and there, Cress had seen, the road stopped. It didn't climb on further into the brown, cactus-covered, snake-inhabited foothills, but ended in a loop among the derricks at the hill's top.

And, though the settlement was on a hillside, Cress always thought of it as being in a dark pocket. It *was* dark there, not only because the earth was oil-soaked and pocked with sump holes that shone like greasy bruises in the gray dust, but because the oil people, wishing for something green amid the barren forests of their derricks, had planted, years ago, pepper trees along their streets. Now that the trees were old, their foliage sprayed outward in dense, smothering cascades, setting the oil workers' homes in gloomy caverns of shade. And it was dark there because the hill blotted the sun out early; while children in the valley below still played in the slanting light of afternoon, the houses of the oil workers would already be deep in evening shadows.

The sun, going down behind a Kettle Hill derrick, sometimes seemed to Cress, watching from her own back steps in the valley, to set it ablaze for a second. She had often seen real flames there when a gusher, coming in with force, blew its casing head and caught on fire. Then, until the flames were quenched, Kettle Hill would look like a fiery torch held up toward the night sky, and gas pockets, exploding, would rattle valley windows with a doomsday sound. And even when all was going quietly on Kettle Hill, it was not really quiet there. Day and night, the throb and stomp of its engines, the sullen, hollow suck of its pumps filled the air. The sound was so constant that days went by when Cress did not hear it at all; then suddenly, in the dead of night, she would be awakened by it, sit bolt upright, and ask herself, "What is that terrible sound?"

"Ina can't help living there," Cress said to her mother accusingly. "Where your folks are, there you have to be."

"Why, I never said she could help it," Mrs. Delahanty answered. "I never even suggested she would want to help it. And I think it would be a very nice thing for you to visit her."

Cress didn't know whether it would be a nice thing or not, but anyway the matter was now decided. She was going.

She felt very lonely, packing. On the evening before the day she was to leave, she started putting together what she would need for her visit. She was using a little satchel of her father's as an overnight bag. It was small enough not to be awkward to carry to school on the bus. She was packing things she couldn't possibly need, because in her mind the trip was somehow momentous. She had made a list and was checking off articles on it, like an overseas traveler. Her father watched her awhile from the doorway of her room. "Cress," he asked, "have you drawn up your will and taken out travel insurance?"

Cress looked up from the midst of the articles she was checking: bottles containing iodine, camphorated oil, attar of roses, hand balm, green ink; a package of band-aids; a comb cleaner, which she had never used in the two years she had owned it; a spray of lavender tied with frayed silver gauze and fast breaking down into lavender dust; a little book bound in purple suède and called "Flowers from Tennyson."

"Let's see," said her father. "Just how long is it you're to be away from us?"

"Till Thursday," said Cress bleakly.

"A whole day?" Mr. Delahanty asked. "Are you taking a calendar with you? I wouldn't want you to lose track of time while you're away."

Cress knew her father was being funny and she tried to smile, but her face seemed to have lost all of its springiness. It seemed to be nothing more than flesh loosely covering the front of her head and useless for purposes of expression.

She folded a hair net of her mother's and put it in the satchel.

"Crescent," Mr. Delahanty said, "I bet a witch doctor in the heart of Africa couldn't have a crazier mess of junk than you've got there."

Cress nodded, but couldn't explain. She felt as if she might be an entirely different person when she got to Ina's —but different in just what way, she couldn't now tell. If, after she arrived, she were to find herself, suddenly, the kind of person who wasn't at home without a hair net, she would wish she had a hair net with her.

Her father watched her awhile longer. "You give me the creeps," he said finally, and walked on down the hall.

Cress nodded to herself after her father left. That was just how she felt. Creepy. She crept about the rooms, slyly picking up things, as if she were stealing them. Stealing from whom, she wondered. Herself? Stealing from the room, she guessed. She took her little flowered calendar from the wall, drew a circle around Thursday, May 20th, and put the calendar on top of everything else in the satchel. Then, as she noticed the small, unfaded spot it left on the wallpaper, tears came to her eyes.

"Look here, Crescent," her mother said, coming into the room. "You know you don't have to visit your friend Ina if you don't want to. No one's forcing you to go, you know."

"Oh, I want to go!" cried Cress intensely. "Besides," she added, "I feel it's Fated."

"Fated," repeated Mrs. Delahanty. "Well, in that case, I guess there's nothing more to be said."

"No," said Cress in a voice of resignation, "I guess not," and closed her father's satchel with a snap.

Next evening, when Cress got off the school bus at the foot of the hill with Ina, she was in a mood to be a perfect guest and to see the best in Kettle Hill. For one thing, she felt contrite. She had talked to some of the girls that day at school rather as if her visit to Ina were a slumming trip.

"Going to see how the other half lives," she had said, and listened to the appreciative laughter. When the girls had asked her what she had in her valise, she had said, "My crude-oil-colored week-end wardrobe, so I won't spot," and was rewarded with laughter again.

If she had said these things in front of Ina, it wouldn't have been so bad, but she hadn't; she had been two-faced, said them behind Ina's back, and the girls had still been snickering when Ina came up to them. The memory of this two-facedness made a sore spot in her chest and, as she climbed the street under the pepper trees, caused her to link her arm through Ina's.

"It's a ratty little town," Ina said apologetically.

"Why, it's not either," said Cress, putting balm on the sore spot. "I think it's romantic."

In a way, a peculiar way, it really was. The fading sunlight came through chinks in the pepper trees and fluttered about upon the hard-packed earth, like a covey of yellow evening birds. The houses, though small, and almost all

alike, because they were company-owned, were neat and
whitewashed. Their porches were filled with large potted
plants growing in cheerful red Hills Brothers coffee cans,
or with smaller potted plants in green Del Monte peach
cans. In some of the houses, the shades were drawn, for
here people worked on shifts and one man's night might
be his neighbor's day. A picket fence, also whitewashed,
ran the length of the street, and each man had a private
gate to his yard, weighted in such a manner with old
springs and defunct batteries that it swung shut of itself
and he need never give a thought to its closing. From
under the pepper trees, the derricks were out of sight. It
was only the smell of the oil—which was taste as much as
smell—the sight of an occasional sump hole at the end of
a side street, and the sound of the pumps that reminded
Cress where she was. The sound of the pumps filled the
air, deep, rhythmical, as if the hills themselves breathed;
or as if deep in the wells some kind of heart shook the
earth with so strong a beat that Cress could feel it in the
soles of her feet as she walked along. Ina seemed not to
hear the sound at all, and Cress felt it as much as she heard
it. When she put out her hand to touch the palings of the
fence, the sound was there, too. In the dead wood were
tremblings which seemed almost alive and which kept time
with the deep, solemn beat of the pumps. This trembling,
this sound that she felt in the soles of her feet and the palm
of her hand, excited Cress.

"There's a book in the library," she said, "called *The
Romantic Story of Oil.*"

"Is there really?" said Ina. Ina had worn one of her best dresses to school, showing how important she thought Cress's visit—a soft silk pongee middy suit. She stopped beside Cress now and clasped her pongee-colored hands. "Cress Delahanty," she said, "I think you are the most sweet and tactful girl I know. Oh, I could just about hug you for that!" she said, reaching out and taking Cress's hand inside her own soft, folding palm. "Most people," she confided, "just see the oil, and smell the smells, and miss the romance."

"Most people," said Cress, working her fingers out of Ina's hand, "are blind."

For some reason, Ina took her into the house by the back door. She said, "Here we are," and Cress, carrying her bulging valise, stepped over the threshold and into the kitchen.

There she was, at the end of her journey, and she looked about to see where that was; she was in a small, very neat room, she saw at once, the table ready set for supper, and chairs standing in front of each place. The room was close, with the smell a kitchen has which is left each morning the minute breakfast is finished and is not re-entered again until evening. The smell of breakfast coffee was still there, and another smell, as if in some cupboard a sack of potatoes had first sprouted, then rotted.

Cress had never seen a more orderly room. Over the sink, can openers, egg beaters, potato mashers—all the kitchen implements—were hung with careful regard for their size, tapering away from the big articles at the sink's

edge to the small ones near the faucets. Half a lemon
rested in the exact center of a saucer, and the saucer had
been placed in the exact middle of the window sill. The
chairs, ranged around the set table, were all pushed under
it a uniform distance, and on the back of the stove was a
stack of pot holders, the largest at the bottom, so that they
formed a pyramid, calculated and orderly.

The room was orderly in the way a sickroom is orderly,
or the room of a person who has little time or is for some
reason unsure of himself. It reminded Cress of a house
she had seen somewhere, a house she could only half remember. Then, suddenly, she remembered it altogether—
the home of a blind friend of her mother's, a woman who
had to depend solely upon her sense of touch to find what
she wanted.

Ina, as if she knew what Cress was thinking, said,
"Father likes everything very neat. He says he wants to
be able to put out his hand in the dark and find whatever
he wants."

Cress saw Ina looking at her, trying to discover if this
seemed strange to her. "I expect I'm messy," Cress said.

"Oh, no!" Ina protested, leading the way into the living
room. "That's the last thing I'd think of calling you."

Cress paused in the doorway to the living room. "Why,
it's nice!" she exclaimed, and then worried for fear the
surprise she felt had shown in her face or voice.

She had somehow thought of Kettle Hill homes as being
faded, run-down, and dingy inside. This room was none
of these things; it was a small, warmly colored, padded-

looking room, as if, Cress thought, the Walleniuses had turned a footstool wrong side out and set up housekeeping in it. It bulged softly toward her as she stood in the doorway; its innumerable curves reached out to touch her. Chairs were plump, the pillows round and solid as boulders; lamps had egg-shaped bases; the phonograph of red, shining wood bellied out about the middle, as if swollen with the volume of sound it contained; even the rug, as she stepped into the room, was not flat but rose in a flowery fuzz under her feet; and the white lace curtains inclined toward her as if by pressure of a hand or face from outside.

The light, already dimmed by its passage through the pepper trees, was dimmed once again before it got into the room through these curtains, and Cress was startled when her eyes, coming to the room's final dark corner, saw that a man whom she knew by his resemblance to Ina to be Mr. Wallenius had been very calmly looking at her while she had been looking at the room. He hadn't been reading or dozing; he wasn't sitting slumped, resting in his chair. He sat bolt upright, calmly watching the two of them, and when Cress's eyes discovered him, he rose very politely and spoke.

"Good evening, girls."

When Mr. Wallenius stood up, Cress saw that he was a large man, broad as well as tall, old but only old like a father, not like a grandfather, as the Bible reading had led her to believe. His hair was yellow white, like Ina's, not silvery with age, and he had a yellow-white mustache, very thick and soft-looking.

"This is my friend Cress Delahanty, Father," Ina said, and Cress shrank inside herself a little at seeing how proud Ina was to have a friend.

"Cress," said Mr. Wallenius. He had a pink-and-white skin, not a loose, golden one like his daughter's, but his voice, Cress thought, had rather a loose, golden sound, like a handful of rings clinked softly together.

"Well, well," said Mr. Wallenius, "so I'm to have two cooks tonight instead of one." Then, reaching out both hands, Mr. Wallenius spread open his fingers so that they circled the top of each girl's head. He did not let his hands rest there, heavy and inert, but moved his long, muscular fingers, so that Cress could feel her scalp being pushed gently this way and that across the top of her skull.

"With the two of you," he said, "I'm going to expect something extra special this evening. I'm going to look forward to something out of the ordinary."

Then, with a final pleasant twitch of their scalps, Mr. Wallenius took his hands from their heads and Cress heard him presently spitting and splashing in the bathroom as he brushed and washed for supper.

Supper-getting was very simple because Ina had planned it so carefully. Before she had gone to school that morning, she had boiled potatoes and made white sauce. Now she diced the potatoes and put them, together with pink, rubbery cubes of bologna, into the pan of white sauce and set the mixture on the stove. While this—whatever it was called—heated, she opened a can of beets, set them to cooking, too, and got a bowl of deviled eggs out of the icebox.

When the food was ready and they had carried it, dished up on three plates, to the table, Ina said proudly, "I tried to have different colors, and the hot food hot and the cold food cold."

Cress thought she had succeeded very well; the bologna-potato mixture was pink and white, the beets a dark, handsome crimson, the deviled eggs, in their green nests of lettuce leaves, gray and yellow. Steam rose above the helpings of heated food; the eggs shone with a cold and clammy sweat.

But the cold food was warmer and the hot food much cooler before they ate, for Mr. Wallenius came into the kitchen, clean and damp from his brushing and scrubbing, just as they put the plates on the table, and asked, "Will you read for us tonight, Miss Cress?" and placed an opened Bible in her hands. After they took their places, Cress read the chapter through. She was accustomed to the Bible and knew that it was right for her to speak aloud words found there which, elsewhere, it would be very wrong for her to whisper or even think about. So she was able to finish without stumbling or blushing, though she couldn't help feeling the chapter was a funny one to have chosen to be read aloud. Then she thought that perhaps the Walleniuses were reading the Bible straight through and did not think it right to pick and choose among God's words.

After the reading was finished and they had begun to

eat, Mr. Wallenius asked, "Did you understand what you read?"

Cress wasn't sure whether she had or hadn't. If she said yes, she thought, she might be asked to explain, so she said, "No."

"Ah, so," said Mr. Wallenius. "An old-fashioned home, I expect. Your friend here, Ina, has been long instructed."

Ina got up just then to put the tea on to steep and Cress ate steadily while she was gone, her face low over her plate. The clock in the living room struck half past five and she remembered how early that seemed at home—still afternoon—while here it was already evening, supper half finished, and night not far distant. At home, her father would be just coming in from the orchard, the slanting sunlight making golden the dust that swirled up about his horse's feet; her mother would be at the end of the drive-way, picking up the evening paper and carrying a tidbit of news from it to her father in the barn before she went back into the house to put supper on.

It was strange to think that if the clock here and the one at home were both right (or both wrong in the same way), they were striking this half hour together. Thinking of both clocks, Cress felt herself to be a kind of meeting place for two varieties of time, home time and visiting time. Remembering home, these things seemed stranger than they had even on first sight: the half lemon on the window sill had, in the kitchen's growing duskiness, a sort of misted light of its own; outside, the long, dangling leaves of the pepper trees moved together with the sound of dry fingers

meeting; the faucet at the sink went drip, drip, drip, and
Crescent thought of that falling movement and that sound
never stopping, day after day, inside the silent, closed
house. At stove and sink, Ina was a long time setting the
tea to steep, and the slight clatter she made sounded distant
and muffled—measured, too, as if Ina were listening for
the thump, thump of the wells and spacing her movements
to keep time with theirs.

"Have you ever been kissed?" Mr. Wallenius asked
suddenly. Cress knew at once that he didn't mean by relatives or girls. Keeping her eyes on her plate, she said,
"No."

Finally, looking up, Cress saw that while Mr. Wallenius' eyes were blue, like Ina's, they were not at all
murky, but had instead a shining glaze, like varnish, across
their blueness.

"You're big enough, you know," Mr. Wallenius said,
smiling.

"I guess it goes more by age than size," Cress said miser-
ably, and was glad that just then Ina came to the table
with the tea and dessert, and that there was no more talk
of kissing.

When they rose from the table, Mr. Wallenius said to
his daughter, "I'll take Cress out for a little walk while
you do the dishes, Ina."

Cress's heart sank. "I wouldn't feel right, not helping,"
she said.

"Washing them alone," Mr. Wallenius told her, "is a

little punishment I planned for Ina. A little reminder. Isn't that true, Ina?"

"Yes," said Ina, almost under her breath, and went quickly about the clearing up, so Cress could see no polite way of escaping the invitation. Mr. Wallenius put his hat on his head and took from behind the door to the living room a knotted and burly stick.

"In case we come across a snake or two," he said as they went down the kitchen steps. "I enjoy killing those fellows."

This made Cress feel better—a walk with a purpose, not just wandering about in the dusk with an almost total stranger.

"I killed a rattlesnake once," she told him.

"How?" asked Mr. Wallenius.

"Stoned it," said Cress.

"I can think of better ways."

So could Cress, but when you were alone and barefoot, what other way was there?

"My father shoots their heads off," she said.

"You find many down there in the groves?"

"Not so many any more," Cress said.

"They slide down the main street here, as much at home as the oldest inhabitants," Mr. Wallenius said. "I guess they are the oldest inhabitants. They lift their heads up and give you the once-over as they pass by. Maybe I'll have a chance to show you."

Cress, who had hunted snakes herself and knew how

scarce they were when looked for, thought the chances for
this were slim, though she was too polite to say so. They
came out from under the pepper trees, where the air had
been hot and close, and turned down a side street. Overhead, the sky, which they could now see, still held considerable light and there was a streak of muddy yellow above
the hills to show where the sun had set. At the bottom of
the street, they came to a sump hole—not one of the big
ones, no more than an eye, liquid and dark, reflecting the
sky. It shimmered iridescently where water had seeped in
with the oil and rose upward here and there in bubbles, as
if it were an eye that could breathe as well as see.

Mr. Wallenius stirred it a little with the point of his
stick, then went off to poke about among the straggling
trees and bushes that grew at the sump hole's upper edges.

Sump holes always made Cress uneasy, whether they
were large ponds or only small, ragged pools like this one.
It seemed unnatural to find a pool of oil instead of water
in the ground. This one was stranger than most, because,
lying at the foot of a little arroyo down which there was
a trickle of water in the winter months, it had stunted
willows and elders, dusty castor-bean and tobacco-plant
shrubs growing about it, like a real pond of water. Several
birds, having seen the light reflected in it and mistaken it
for water and dipping too low, had died there. Dragonflies
and moths had darted down to drink and never risen again.
It was a very strange place, yet peaceful—no sounds except
the pumps, the dry, placid singing of insects in the faded

grass, and Mr. Wallenius' quiet poking about in the elder clump. It was half pleasant, half frightening, standing there—frightening to think that if she were as easily fooled as a bird or dragonfly, she, too, could plunge in and not come out; pleasant to think that though she stood on the edge of danger, she was safe because she saw it.

"Ah, ha!" cried Mr. Wallenius. "What did I tell you?"

He came out of the elder clump with a heavy snake hanging across his walking stick. Fearful of falling, the snake balanced itself there, its head slightly lifted, its tongue flicking in and out so quickly that in the dusk it almost seemed that a vapor came from its mouth.

Cress jumped quickly backward as Mr. Wallenius advanced. Then she saw, even in the fading light, that what he had picked up was nothing more than a poor gopher snake that had probably been out hunting a mouse for supper.

"It's nothing but a gopher snake," she said. "Nothing but a poor, harmless gopher snake."

"A fine fellow," Mr. Wallenius replied, as if agreeing. "Fat and sassy. I'll just put him in here to cool off a bit."

Then, with a gentle movement, Mr. Wallenius laid, rather than threw, the soft, brown, harmless thing in the sump hole.

Cress could not believe her eyes. So terrible a thing to do! Involuntarily, she took hold of Mr. Wallenius' wrist. "It will die," she told him.

"Maybe so, maybe not," said Mr. Wallenius. "It's too

early to say. Sink—swim; sink—swim," he said. "Sink—swim."

It was almost as if the snake heard and obeyed. Oil-covered, eyes blinded, tongue motionless, it struggled, it rose and sank, rose and sank.

"Sink—swim," said Mr. Wallenius. "Up—down; in—out."

Behind the blunt, striving, blinded head making its horrible effort to rise, yet falling back again, the snake's body moved with such energy that against anything with less resistance than oil it would have broken free. But the oil held like fingers. Along the whole of her body, Cress felt the terror and effort of that struggle—the oil in her own eyes, the taste of oil in her own mouth.

"Save him!" she implored. "Save him! It's wicked to do that. It hurts him so!"

"Sink—swim," said Mr. Wallenius. "Sink—swim."

A bird darted near the surface of the sump hole, then flashed away; the evening insects sang on; there was a little flurry of wind among the elder leaves.

"Sink—swim," said Mr. Wallenius. "Under—out."

The snake's head lifted and fell; it kept time, it seemed, not only with the words Mr. Wallenius spoke but with the thud and suck of the pumps and with the rhythmical pressure of Mr. Wallenius' fingers on Cress's hand, which she now realized he was holding.

"It's dying!" Cress cried, her shrill voice disturbing all that orderly time-keeping going on so relentlessly about the sump hole, and, weeping not only for the snake but for herself, she plunged away from Mr. Wallenius and began, desperately, to run.

The last half-mile down the spur line, she walked, and she had stopped crying a mile or so before that. By the time she stood on her own front porch, she had stopped catching her breath, too, and had wiped her face fairly clean with the bottom of her skirt.

It was so natural to be there and to see her mother and father sitting by the open window talking, that everything else, the whole visit—orderly kitchen, lemon that shone like a light, sweating eggs, snake, sump hole, even Mr. Wallenius—seemed objects she might have imagined in the two minutes between stepping outside to see the stars and going back into the house again. But when she opened the screen door, she realized that she had actually been away, for her mother, very startled, jumped from her chair and said, "Why, Cress Delahanty, how on earth do you happen to be here now?"

Cress didn't know what answer to make. It seemed foolish to say, "Because Mr. Wallenius drowned a snake in a sump hole." She thought of saying, "Because it's Fated, I guess," but that wasn't true. What had been Fated was for her to spend the night at the Walleniuses'. She had broken that by running.

"I guess I was homesick," she finally said.

She saw her father and mother look at each other. Her father stood up. "Well," he said, "I'm glad you were. And you didn't get here a minute too soon. I was just on the point of putting us together some kind of a bedtime snack. How does that sound to you?"

It sounded good, but Cress was silent. She sat down in her father's chair and nodded yes to him, because suddenly she was too tired to speak even so small and easy a word.

PART III
Fourteen

Early Summer

The sun blazed, fledglings flew, roses bloomed. But there was still, for Southern California, an indication of a lingering spring: green grass. There had been late rains and the yellow look had not yet come to the foothills and the grass in the Delahanty back yard was still February fresh. Now in late afternoon each bent blade carried on its hump a drop of water left over from the midday shower. The low sun, slanting through these drops, gave them jewel colors and Crescent, walking toward the house, put her feet down carefully. She was now fourteen years old and oppressed by the brevity of life, the fugaciousness of blossoms, and the evanescence of raindrops. Even words like evanescent and fugacious could set up, with their suggestive syllables, delicious tremors of sorrow in her heart. Ending, ending, everything is ending, she thought. In spite of her care, raindrops like emeralds and diamonds went flying down to nothing as she walked. She was even sorrowful about the box of tin cans she had just taken to the stack behind the barn. She had put them down with benedictory thoughts: finished and done with!

Gone from the orderly kitchen shelves and the bright
lights of the house into the cold earth.

There were tears in her eyes as she walked through
the grass. She had more feelings than she knew what to
do with, more emotions than her tranquil life permitted
her to discharge. She had to invent sorrows and concoct
dramas. She would stoop down to rejoice with a daffodil
that had pushed a stone aside in its upward thrust, or
would loosen a butterfly from a spider web with wailings
that brought her no sympathy from any listener. As if she
cared for sympathy! She was capable emotionally of a
woman's tragedies and, up to now, she had been unable
to overtake any of these. Now, however, she loved and
was not loved in return. No one, not even Calvin Dean,
knew anything of this; though she could not believe it
would matter if he did. That was a part of his appeal:
his indifference. He didn't know Crescent Delahanty existed. Why should he?

With rubies and emeralds and diamonds transformed
by her feet into simple raindrops and the raindrops themselves shattered into the shapelessness of moisture she
thought, I'm King Midas in reverse. I change jewels to
water. I can touch gold and make it into a base metal, lead
or tin. She stood ankle deep in the diamonds and rubies
she had yet to ruin and figured what her name was. Midas
in reverse was Sadim. I am King Sadim, she told herself,
and the jewels I touch are water and the gold I touch is
dust and the people I love hate me.

With these thoughts, she went into the kitchen, which

was warm and fragrant with the tamale pie her mother was making. Her mother was at the sink shaking olives from a bottle. Cress watched her for a second or two, then said, "I am King Sadim."

Her mother, who did not turn around, asked in a cheerful voice, "Who's King Sadim, dear?"

"King Midas had a brother and Sadim was his name," Cress said, the relationship coming to her as she spoke.

"I never heard of him," Mrs. Delahanty replied. "I didn't know King Midas had a brother."

"This brother was not popular. He was King Midas in reverse. Everything he touched turned into dust. It may be bad to have everything you touch turn to gold—but it's a lot better than having everything you touch turn to dust. Nobody liked King Sadim and everybody tried to forget him. I may be the only person in the world who remembers him."

Her mother, who had the olives out of the bottle, now began to stir them into her pie. She looked up from her stirring with amused interest, as Cress related this bit of unknown mythology. Cress regarded her mother dispassionately. The rain and the steam in the kitchen had made her new permanent too frizzy. There was a big splash of cornmeal mush across her apron. Her lipstick formed a dot at each corner of her mouth. She was smiling quite happily. Happy, Cress thought, on a spring evening of unutterable beauty, with nothing better to do than make a tamale pie. A pie that will be eaten tonight and forgotten tomorrow.

"Oh, Mother," she cried. "Poor, poor Mother." She dug an olive out of the pie and put it into her mouth. Under her closed lids she felt the happy smart of tears saying, You are alive and suffering. She took the olive seed from her mouth and pushed it deep into the well-watered soil about one of the African violet plants which her mother kept in pots along the window sill over the sink.

"What are you doing, Cress?" her mother asked.

"Giving it one more chance," Cress whispered, patting the soil in tenderly over the buried seed.

"Giving what one more chance?"

"The olive seed. It had given up. Into the bottle, into the pie, into my mouth. Like Jonah. Then when it thought all was over I spat it up. Rescue. Escape. It will be a tree again."

"It never was a tree, Cress. Any more than an egg ever was a chicken."

"It is an embryonic tree, Mother. It has leaves and limbs locked in its heart." All those surprising l's. *They* brought tears to her eyes, too.

"Leave them locked," Mrs. Delahanty said unfeelingly. "I don't want leaves and limbs in my kitchen. I want African violets."

"O.K.," Cress said, "if that's the way you feel about it." She began disinterring the seed. "The choice is yours. Life or Death. You choose Death." She opened the window over the sink and flung the olive pit out into the

April twilight. "Die," she bade it in a tragic voice. "Cease to be. It is my mother's wish."

Her mother slid the tamale pie into the oven. "How much death do you think there is in that tamale pie, Mother?" Cress asked.

Her mother looked startled and Cress said, "One cow at the very least. Two maybe."

"Cress," her mother said, "you have a bad case of spring fever. You need some vitamins or minerals or something."

Death in the world, spring passing, love never coming, and vitamins were recommended.

"Do you *know* it's spring?" Cress asked. "That this is a day that will never again be upon this earth? Never, never, never? And that it's the last day on earth a lot of people will ever see? There," she said, pointing to the fragment of pale sun still visible through the darkening leaves of the eucalyptus tree, "that sun is going down forever for someone at this very minute."

Something came into her mother's face, agreement, she was afraid. And she couldn't bear agreement or understanding just now. What she longed for was sorrow and contention, lasting disorder and sudden death. She ran out of the kitchen slamming the door behind her. In her own room she flung herself onto the chair in front of her bamboo desk, put her arms on the open lid of the desk and her face on her arms. "Oh, Calvin," she whispered. Then, very daringly, "My darling." The word made a pulse beat on her cheekbone.

She reached out a hand and began to pat the frayed straw matting with which her desk was covered. The desk was her dearest possession. She had bought it from the Second Hand Furniture Mart with $11.98 of her own money. It had come to the Furniture Mart from a beach cottage and it still smelled of seaweed and salt water, with an occasional whiff of Djer Kiss and grunnion. Its stork-thin legs were stained and wobbly. It was everywhere lightly pocked with what appeared to be old buckshot wounds but which were actually worm holes. She liked it that way. She would not have cared for unscarred varnish fresh from a furniture factory. "Oh, desk," she said. She felt it was her real home.

Once when she was a child, her real home for over a year had been the piano box in which their new piano had come and which had stood out behind the barn. She slept in the house of course and ate there—but as a boarder, as a matter of convenience. Her real home was the piano box. She had sat in it, feet curled beneath her, rain falling like a beaded curtain across its opening, and speculated about the people who lived up at the Delahanty house. What kind of people were they? Did they have any children? She would have to call on them some day.

She couldn't get into her desk, of course, as she had the piano box, but it was, in the same way, her home. She sat up now, so vigorously the desk rocked, and took from one of its pigeonholes a fold of adding-machine paper given her by the manager of the Piggly Wiggly store. She unfolded the long strip of paper, looked over

what was already written there, picked up her pen and
began where she had left off: "39. I love Calvin Dean.
40. I love Calvin Dean. 41. I love Calvin Dean." When
she had written "I love Calvin Dean" one hundred times
she intended to fold the paper to the size of a postage
stamp and put it in the little chamois bag her mother had
once used to carry her rings in. Then she would hang
this bag around her neck, on a ribbon the right length
to keep the words exactly over her heart. She would wear
it night and day, in water or out (wrapped in oiled paper
and held in her mouth on these occasions). She would
never be parted from it; she would stand in Calvin Dean's
presence, every thud of her heart lifting the words, "I
love Calvin Dean," written one hundred times over, a
fraction of an inch nearer him. Surely he would feel it,
surely it would influence him.

She paused at "56. I love Calvin Dean" to think about
him. He was eighteen years old, a big ruddy boy, blond-
haired and supple. She thought he probably looked like
Charlemagne and, like Charlemagne, he seemed born to
command. He was the head of everything at school that
had a head, from captain of the football team to president
of the debating club.

Because of Calvin she had suffered agonies of shyness
and hard work to win a place on the debating team. She
was now first substitute and should any misfortune ever
overtake Connie Bielefeldt, Calvin's partner, she herself
would have to debate with Calvin, a possibility so overwhelming she tried not to think of it. Her try-out speech

on the negative side of socialized medicine had been
against her conscience, but since every word of it had been
the truest cry of her heart, "Calvin see me, Calvin hear
me," it had not been really hypocritical. And Calvin had
seen and heard. And momentarily, and partially anyway,
he had approved, for he had voted for her as first substitute.

Making the debating team had put her nearer Calvin,
but this nearness had made her no more happy. His
presence was too overwhelming. When the debating club
met and Calvin presided she would fix her eyes on the
picture of Longfellow which hung at the front of the
room to keep from staring at Calvin. At the end of the
meeting her eyes would be so tired from this enforced
exploration of the curlicues in Longfellow's whiskers, that
she would have to go to the girl's rest room to bathe
them. Once in the middle of a meeting Calvin had stopped
the proceedings to address her directly. "Would you mind
telling us," he had asked, "what you see in that picture,
anyway?"

"Me?" she had whispered, nudged by a neighbor from
her cultivated inattention.

Calvin had turned his back on the debating club to gaze
up at Longfellow. Facing Cress again he had said, "I don't
see the likeness myself."

"Oh no," Cress had explained as the laughter quieted,
"I don't mean I see me in the picture." And too shaken
for anything but the most literal truth she said, "What
I mean is I don't see you."

Calvin had given her, at this, his long cold debater's stare with which he was wont to impress judges and paralyze opponents. "Delahanty," he said, practicing his university manner, "are you crazy?"

From too shy she had gone to too bold. The desk under her arms shook as she remembered what she had said. Determined to say something and unable to think of anything but synonyms for "crazy" she had rolled them all off: "Crazy," she had agreed, "demented, mad, irresponsible, tetched, nuts, moonstruck, bats in my belfry, off my trolley, lunatic . . ."

If Calvin had not interrupted her she might have gone on indefinitely. "In a word," he had said, "crazy."

That had been his last word to her: "Crazy." She picked up her pen and wrote, to forget it, "57. I love Calvin Dean. 58. I love Calvin Dean."

At "59. I love—," her mother without a knock or a whistle came into the room. "Studying, Cress?" she asked.

"No," Cress answered. She didn't put away or try to hide her Piggly Wiggly strip of paper. In a way she did not understand, she wished her mother would pick it up, read it, and ask: "What's the meaning of all this 'I love Calvin Dean,' Cress?"

Then she would answer, tell her everything, say: "The meaning is, I love Calvin Dean and he doesn't know I exist except to think I'm crazy." It would be an excuse, if her mother picked it up, to tell her everything, of all the miseries of her life. How sad it was to die and to be a debater and to love the most outstanding boy in school and to destroy emeralds and diamonds. Tell her and ask her, "What's the matter with me? Why am I so sad and miserable? Why do I turn things into dust?"

But her mother, very honorably averted her eyes from the list and asked, diffidently: "I don't suppose you'd want to ride into town with us, would you?"

There was a time—could it be only last fall—when she would have been the first one out in the car at that invitation. But it was a dream-like time, vanished, remembered like a dream. "No," she said. "Thanks just the same, but I guess not."

Her mother lingered. Finally she said, "If your mind's made up I won't urge. Keep your eye on the tamale pie, will you?" Then, as if she had perhaps been too quick to accept Cress's refusal she turned back from the door. "Oh come on, Cress. It's a beautiful evening. We're just going in and back. Your father has to pick up something from the garage for the tractor. We won't be gone a minute. The tamale pie can take care of itself. Come on."

"No," Cress said, "I guess not."

"You used to love trips to town."

"I know I did."

"But not now?"

"Not tonight."

"Want us to bring you anything?"

"There's nothing I want you can buy."

"O.K.," her mother said. "Good-by then. We're going as soon as your father washes up."

When the door closed she began her writing again.

"59. I love Calvin Dean. 60. I love Calvin Dean. 61. I love Calvin Dean." Her pen, as she remembered momentarily those trips to town, faltered. There was first of all the pleasure of the change from the quiet of the ranch to the movement and noise of the city. After a week at the ranch storekeepers, carrying in at closing time the baskets of yams and cabbages from the sidewalk, seemed exciting. They would bulge out their white-aproned stomachs to form a shelf on which to rest a lug of tomatoes. They would call out to passers-by: "Haven't seen you for a coon's age," or "How's tricks?" Weighed down with what they were carrying, they would take short housewifely steps, and the pencils behind their ears would tremble a little.

She remembered the library, empty usually at this time of everyone but herself, the librarian and two old men reading papers, the four of them sealed away from the world among the books, a spell of silence put upon them forever. She remembered the hollow engulfed-cathedral echo of the six o'clock chimes from the Presbyterian church as it was absorbed and deadened by the rows of books.

She remembered the trip home from town, the library books on the back seat (among them perhaps the best book of her life). She remembered the hot buttered popcorn which the three of them ate while they speculated about the people, fragments of whose lives were revealed to them through their lighted windows. Remembering all these pleasures they did not, after all, seem past. They *were* pleasure and they were hers right now for the taking.

She ran out of her room, down the hall, and through the dining room crying, "I've changed my mind." The car was just backing out of the driveway and she ran on-to the side porch shouting, "Wait for me. I've changed my mind." But she was too late. They didn't hear her. The car rolled smoothly away without a sign from either of them. They were laughing and talking, with not the least memory it appeared of her. No one looking at them would guess that they were driving off, leaving their only child alone while they went merrymaking.

She went back into the empty house, into her empty room, and there without bothering to sit down, picked up her pen and wrote "62. I love Calvin Dean."

What was she doing standing at her bamboo desk, writing "I love you" one hundred times to a boy who didn't know she existed? She was suddenly alone, not only in the house, but in the world.

"I am alone in the world," she said and the words had a terrible ring of truth which she had never intended.

Summer I

That summer, Cress became a great lover of signs and portents—the summer she was fourteen, when everything was changing. Signs and portents didn't stop the changes, didn't even slow them down, but they did forewarn her. That was something. It was something to know that if you laughed before breakfast you would cry before supper, that Friday would be either the fairest or the foulest day of the week, that a pointed elbow is the certain sign of a sour disposition, and that a sweating glass brings rain.

Cress started her days that summer by counting buttons and ended them by counting one-eyed autos. One-eyed autos were called padiddles that summer, no one knew why. In between times, she counted white horses, loads of hay, tea leaves, bridges, beards, and mules. She wished on falling stars, over running water, and upon making accidental rhymes.

"Spit," she yelled at her father when a jack rabbit ran in front of their car.

Mr. Delahanty had learned that summer to spit first and reason later. "Why?" he asked, having spat.

"We'd been sure to've had a blowout if you hadn't."

Cress was shocked when her mother threw half of a too large pinch of salt into the sink.

"All the salt you throw away," Cress told her mother, "you have to come back after you're dead and pick up with your eyelashes."

Mrs. Delahanty rinsed away the salt that still remained on her hand. "Cress," she asked, "you don't really believe all this nonsense, do you?"

Wary as a witch doctor, Cress replied, "Why take a chance?" and continued her propitiations.

That was the summer Cress saw Honor Gallagher again after Honor had been away a year, a meeting that didn't surprise Cress. Hadn't it been foretold? Hadn't she dropped the dishcloth, dreamed of running water, and the day she saw Honor said her name not once but twice before eating?

> *A name that's spoken before eating*
> *You'll use ere nightfall as a greeting.*

The day she saw Honor again was a Monday, the day after the Fourth of July. Cress came to breakfast late and sat looking at her orange juice, not drinking it. After a day at the beach, she felt too passive and dreamy to eat, even to drink.

"Mother," she said, "is it O.K. with you if I go swimming in the Ditch this afternoon?"

The Ditch, which carried irrigation water to the orange groves, was nicer than it sounded, shoulder deep, wide as a narrow road, curving among the glossy-leaved trees.

"I don't know how you can stand any more water, Crescent," her mother said. Mrs. Delahanty's face, except for large white circles about her eyes, where her sunglasses had protected her, was raspberry-colored, and when she spoke, she tried to move her mouth as little as possible. Cress admired this way of talking. She thought it made her mother look a little like George Raft.

"I wish you could have given me a good, solid name," Cress said, "instead of Crescent."

"What do you mean, good and solid?" Mrs. Delahanty asked.

"Old-fashioned," Cress explained. "Like Faith or Abigail or Prudence."

"I once knew a girl named Abundance," Mr. Delahanty said. Mr. Delahanty, being dark, didn't sunburn and was able to speak heartily. "How'd you like that for a name, Cress?"

"Who did you ever know named Abundance?" asked Mrs. Delahanty, stiff-lipped. She had been brought up in the same town as her husband and thought she knew all the girls he knew.

"Bunny Evans," Mr. Delahanty said.

"So Bunny Evans' name was Abundance." Mrs. Delahanty sounded thoughtful. "I never knew that."

"Abundance is just as bad as Crescent," Cress said. "It's too unusual. My favorite name is Honor. I think it's the most distinguished name I ever heard."

This was not news to Mr. and Mrs. Delahanty. Before

Honor had gone with her parents to Alaska, she had lived
on a ranch adjoining the Delahantys' and had been, in
spite of the five years' difference in their ages, Cress's best
friend.

"Honor *is* a nice name," Mrs. Delahanty said. "But I
like Crescent better. It's more romantic."

"Honor," Cress said, "is solid *and* romantic." Then
she drank her orange juice.

The first thing Cress heard from the other girls when
she got to the Ditch that afternoon was that Honor
Gallagher was back on a visit. Cress hadn't had any letters
from Honor recently. Not that that mattered. After a
lifetime of silence, it would still be the same between her
and Honor.

"Honor and her mother got here Saturday," one of
the girls said. "They're visiting Honor's grandmother, in
town. They've bought a new car and are going to drive
it back to Alaska."

"How swell!" Cress said. "How wonderful!" But all
the time she was floating away from the others, slowly
at first, then faster, around two bends, under Byfield
Bridge, past the clump of acacias, until, finally, she was
alone and, if missed, not missed enough to be shouted at
by anyone or pursued. She drifted on, floating on her back,
and overhead a white cloud like an opened parasol accompanied her. A speckle-backed lady-bug, riding a faded
cottonwood leaf, went with her downstream. The cloud
blotted out the sun, and the water was the color of a

butcher-knife blade; the sun came out and the blade was first polished, then changed from steel to silver. Cress rescued the traveling lady-bug, set her ashore, then anchored herself by an overhanging bank where slanting willows shaded the water.

The water was high. It ran over the grass of the bank, extending it full length, so that it looked like soft, green hair being combed. The shouts of the swimmers were far away, so far that they were no longer human voices but only summery, afternoon sounds. And there were no other sounds at all, except the faraway drone of a tractor endlessly crisscrossing an orchard.

Cress listened and then suddenly began to thrash about, to beat her feet up and down in the water, to squeeze herself as if what she wanted was to be wrung dry. The hair-like grass was washed every which way, and the water, slapping against the bank, was muddied. Then Cress made herself sink to the stream's white, sandy bottom. She opened her eyes underwater and looked at a transformed world. "Honor is home," she thought.

It was at the Ditch that she had first met Honor Gallagher, two years before, the summer she was twelve and Honor seventeen. Cress had been practicing floating then. She could swim but not float. Sinking, as she always did, she looked up and saw a girl in a yellow bathing suit looking down at her from the bank above.

"Let go, let go," the girl above her said, and Cress did so and floated.

Honor was one of the big girls, full grown, one of the

girls Cress had watched from a distance. She had a shape, beautiful, in and out like a flower on a stem. But she was hardy, too, like a boy. There were strong, swelling muscles in her brown legs and arms. When she tautened herself for a dive, two cords stood out in her rounded throat, like cables, like ropes. Her yellow bathing suit was in one piece, not two wisps, like most of the big girls', with vacancies for their bodies to show through. She wore her hair short, turned up all over her head, like waves just ready to break but pausing. Her mouth was pretty. She chewed rose petals lots of times, or sucked nasturtiums for honey, or ate sour grass. She was interested in the tastes of things. "Eyes of gold and bramble-dew," Cress had quoted to her once. It was true but it embarrassed both of them. Honor could swear like a trooper. She was the only girl in the Gallagher family, with older boys on one side of her, younger boys on the other. It was a tussle to stay alive in the midst of them, she used to say.

That first afternoon, she had dived down into the Ditch beside Cress. It takes pains and practice to dive into four feet of water. You can go too straight and break your neck, or flatten out too much and break yourself wide open. Honor went just right—under, then up, in a shallow arc. She had been with the big kids on a swimming party, but it had become a necking party, so she'd left. She stood up in the Ditch, water running down her fierce, pink face. "Those boys! So pinchy, so squeezy!" She opened and closed the fingers of one hand to show what she meant, then dived under again, as if to wash their touch away.

After that, she and Cress were together for a whole year on Saturdays, Sundays, and after school. At first, Cress thought she was too young to be Honor's friend and was apologetic. But Honor liked her as she was. "You're not lovey-dovey," she said once. Well, she had been, really, as far as Honor was concerned, but what Honor meant was that she wasn't lovey-dovey about the boys.

She and Honor had been perfect together. That summer, they had discovered a shallow cave—a ledge with a roof over it, actually, in the hills. There was clean sand on the bottom, two bones—human or animal, neither of them knew which—at the cave's edge, and a view, on clear days, of the ocean. Cress and Honor had gone there that summer at every hour—at sunrise, at sunset, in between. They had imagined, sitting in the cave, that they were the last of the world's survivors. Looking out at the blue lip of the Pacific on the horizon, they had wondered how long it would be before the ocean gnawed inland to them. At other times, they'd imagined themselves to be the first human beings, or visitors from Mars, ignorant of all but their cave and speculating as to what the distant, flashing blue of the Pacific might be.

They had often made fires in their cave and cooked food—hot dogs, usually. Sometimes they had a real meal —roasted potatoes and onions to go with their hot dogs, and served Hostess cupcakes for dessert.

Honor had been memorizing the records of all outstanding batters and pitchers that first summer. She carried with her a small, loose-leaf spiral notebook, a Beacon Wire-o, in which she kept these figures, in her sharp-edged, vertical writing. She would bring her notebook to the cave and get Cress to test her knowledge.

"Why memorize them?" Cress asked her once.

"The mind is a muscle," Honor answered. "I want to exercise mine."

"But why on baseball?"

"I don't want to *guess*, I want to *know* what Lefty Gomez did and the year he did it."

Cress hadn't cared much about Lefty Gomez, but she hadn't been able to help learning about him that summer. What *she* really liked was poetry. She brought an anthology, "Star Points," to the cave, but it was Honor who did all the reading aloud. She could read so much better than Cress, who got carried away by the rhythm and was soon todo-todoing like a player piano. What the words meant was always vivid and clear to Honor, to whom poetry, and even much reading, was new. When she said "stone," the stone would be in her voice, almost in the shape of her mouth; you would imagine you heard it click against her teeth.

When Cress and Honor were not together, they left notes for each other at the Delahanty weir box, which they both passed on their way to catch their respective buses for school. Honor, who went earlier, would find a note put there by Cress the night before, and Cress, at eight-thirty, would pick up a note left there by Honor a half hour before. Honor's notes had been brief and businesslike: "See you tonight 5 P.M. Good luck in Geog. test. H. G." Cress's had been a good deal more flowery. Sometimes she had quoted poetry, sometimes made up some. Once only she had written, "I love you. Crescent Delahanty." Cress had never known what Honor did with her notes. Threw them away, probably; Honor wasn't sentimental. Cress kept all of Honor's, though— she had them yet, in a candy box that looked like a little cedar chest, brass bands, nailheads, and all.

When Honor's father, who, Mr. Delahanty said, was a rolling stone if ever there was one, decided to roll on to Alaska after a year in California, Cress and Honor parted without any schoolgirl protestations of eternal devotion. What was the need? Even their names, Cress thought now as she floated quietly beneath a sky that was empty of clouds, had the sound of names that belonged together: Honor, Crescent—Crescent, Honor. One solid, square, an unchanging rock, the other curving, filled with light, but a reflected light.

Cress was in no great hurry to get home that afternoon. What was the need to rush? Honor would come as soon as she could. She would have to do a certain amount of visiting with her grandmother and other relatives in town; then she would drive out. Cress floated and remembered and dreamed. When, at last, she started home, the sun was low; midges rose and fell above the yellowing road-side weeds. Because she had been in the water so long, her body felt curiously light, washed thin. She was happy about Honor's return, but not excited, she thought. Then, when she saw the new yellow car in the driveway, she knew it was Honor's and began to run.

There was no one on the porch when Cress got there, no one in the living room. She walked into the dining room, paused, and called, "Honor! Honor!"

Mrs. Delahanty came in from the kitchen, wiping her hands on a paper towel. In the shadowy room, her face, which had been almost purple that morning, looked only rosy. "Cress?" she said. "Honor's out in the orchard with your father."

This seemed strange. Honor had never been one to fall in with the boring trips of inspection suggested by grown-ups.

"She wanted to help him pick out some fruit to send back to Alaska," Mrs. Delahanty explained. "Some avocados and grapefruit, and oranges, too, I guess. She wants them to be absolutely perfect."

This was strange, too. Honor had never cared about what she ate. A burned hot dog tasted good to her; she would eat the worm with the apple, if not warned, and never know the difference.

"I'll go find them," Cress said.

"You'd probably just meet them on their way back," Mrs. Delahanty said to her. "Why don't you go brush your hair and put on a clean dress instead? Honor's all dressed up. After all, it's a holiday, you know." Mrs. Delahanty reached out a hand to smooth Cress's hair, which had dried into stiff, finger-width strands.

Cress put on a clean white dress and her new white moccasins, combed her hair, and tied it at the back with a blue ribbon. By the time she had finished, she heard her father's voice and knew that he and Honor had returned from the orchard.

The three of them were sitting about the table when she went into the dining room, a little pyramid of oranges in front of them. Her father was beginning to peel an orange in the methodical way he had, cutting the top off first with his knife.

"Honor," Cress said.

"Hello, Cress," Honor answered, stressing the second syllable of "hello" in a way that was new to her. "How are you, anyway?"

"I'm all right," Cress said. Honor was as beautiful as ever. She had on one of those dresses in two parts, the parts not meeting—a short, tight bodice and a full, swirling skirt. The dress was apricot-colored, and between the bodice and skirt Honor's brown skin was smooth and supple.

"Your mother said you were swimming," Honor remarked politely. "Do you still like to swim?"

"Yes, I do," Cress answered. "I love to. Do you still swim, Honor?"

"Oh, no," Honor answered. "No, not any more." There was a pause in which no one said anything. Then Mrs.

Delahanty said in an interested voice, "I expect you go skiing nowadays, don't you, Honor?"

"Yes," Honor answered, and went on eagerly, "It's so exciting I just can't tell you. It's the nearest thing to flying, they say."

"I was up at Arrowhead at Christmas," Cress said. "I wasn't much good on skis, but I tried."

Honor laughed, shook her head, and then spoke to Mrs. Delahanty. "She hasn't changed, has she?"

I'm right here, Cress thought. You can speak to me, Honor. But Honor went on talking to her mother. Honor, though always polite to older people, used to squirm when Mrs. Delahanty cornered her for five minutes' conversation. Now she was the one who was doing the talking and Mrs. Delahanty the listening. Here I am, Honor, Cress thought, but it was like those movies in which an invisible person tries to communicate with someone. Honor couldn't see her, couldn't hear her voice. She sat near enough to Honor to touch her, but she couldn't do that; there was something that separated them, something transparent and gauze-like that she could see through but couldn't understand and couldn't possibly break.

Mr. Delahanty handed an orange to Honor. "Eat this and see what you've been missing," he told her.

Honor began to peel the orange with her old-time quick, sure gestures. "These are really going to amaze Mike, Mr. Delahanty. I don't think he's ever eaten a tree-ripened orange in his life."

Cress looked inquiringly not at Honor but at her mother.

"Honor's engaged to Mike, dear," her mother said.

"Engaged?" Cress asked, as if it were a word she had never heard.

"To be married," Honor said, smiling, popping the first section of her orange into her mouth.

"When was it you said the wedding was to be?" Mrs. Delahanty asked.

"In September. If Mike gets his leave then."

"Is Mike a soldier?" Cress asked.

"Oh, no, thank God," Honor said. "He's a flier, a commercial flier, but he was in the Army so long he always thinks of vacations as leaves, and so do I, now."

"Two months!" Mrs. Delahanty exclaimed. "That's not long, is it?"

"No, it's really terribly soon," Honor said. "That's the reason Mother and I are down here, actually. To buy me some clothes and get some household equipment. You have an electric stove, don't you, Mrs. Delahanty? Do you think I should get one?"

"I wouldn't have anything else," Mrs. Delahanty said.

"Does yours have its oven and broiler together?"

"Mine does, yes."

"Mike says that wouldn't be too satisfactory. Say you want hot biscuits and a broiled steak at the same time, for instance. How do you manage that?"

"Mike seems to be pretty informed about cooking," Mr. Delahanty observed.

"Oh, Mike knows *everything*," Honor declared.

"Really he does, Mr. Delahanty. Not just cooking—everything."

"And you're going to see that he gets steak and hot biscuits together—this wonder man?" Mr. Delahanty asked.

"Yes, I am," Honor said, refusing to be teased, "if I have to have a stove made to order."

"Why don't you come look at mine?" Mrs. Delahanty suggested. "It's not new, but it's pretty good, I think."

The two women—that was how Cress thought of them now—went out of the room together, and Cress and her father were left alone.

"Sit down, Cress, why don't you?" Mr. Delahanty said.

Cress pulled out one of the chairs from the table and sat down beside her father. It was a nice time of the day, cool after heat, a breeze, newly sprung up, moving the white curtains, enough light yet to put shadows onto the wide oak floorboards.

"Have an orange," Mr. Delahanty said, rolling one toward her. Cress automatically cupped her hand to keep the orange from rolling off the table. She didn't pick it up but moved it back and forth, feeling the warmth that was still in it after a day in the sun. On the table beside the oranges was a card, which said, "Michael J. Gates, Gates's Flying Service, Anchorage, Alaska, Box 1713."

"Is that his name?" Cress asked. "Gates?"

Mr. Delahanty nodded. "It's the address for the fruit."

"How terrible!" Cress said. "How terribly unlucky!"

"Unlucky?" Mr. Delahanty asked.

> "*Change the name and not the letter,*
> *Change for worse and not for better,*"

Cress explained.

But the minute she said the words, Cress knew they didn't matter, and that she would as soon walk under a ladder, throw salt away, put on her left shoe first. All these precautions, all this foresight, all these prophesyings! They were nothing. They were child's play. Countings and wishings and spittings were not going to change anything. In the kitchen she could hear Honor saying, "I should think this deep-well cooker would be pretty economical."

Mr. Delahanty smiled across at her. "There's a calmed-down tomboy for you," he said. "And I suppose it won't be long before you're thinking of steaks and stoves. And Edwin," he added thoughtfully. "How's Edwin," he asked. "I haven't heard you mention him for some time?"

Cress began slowly to peel her orange. She could not think of Edwin now. She could not think ahead to any coming time, only backward to the summer she had first seen Honor and to the summer that for her was already over, the summer of signs and portents.

Summer II

Cress sat a little removed from Yolande Perrotti and Yolande's boy friend, waiting for the magic of the house party to bloom about her. The chief ingredients of that magic, as she had imagined it, were present: the sea and a boy. And though the Pacific, with its waves shattering from glass to foam and from green to white, was behaving as she had expected, Yolande and her boy friend were not.

The boy had come up out of the breakers fifteen minutes ago to join Yolande, and Cress had waited, at first excitedly, then unhappily, for the introduction which never came. Now, magic postponed for a while longer, she lay back on the sand which, though it shimmered warmly with a thousand reflected lights off the broken sea, was cold and clammy to the touch. She put an arm across her eyes and excluded the sight of those who were excluding her.

This was the first day of the house party; in fact, at nine in the morning, almost its first hour. For though they had arrived at the beach at dusk the night before, that flurry of unpacking, of eating peanut-butter sandwiches and making beds could not, surely, be called the "house party," any more than the arranging of a stage is called a

214

play. So perhaps it was too early to judge or condemn the house party because it was so unlike the house party she had imagined, or the girls had planned. Or even the house party her mother had feared. Though all of these parties—the planned, the imagined, and the feared—were alike in one respect: what was most important in all of them had never been mentioned by anyone.

It had taken Cress two weeks to persuade her mother to let her go to the house party at all. At first, Mrs. Delahanty had said no because of Cress's age. At fourteen, she said, a girl was too young to go to a house party. Cress had countered this by naming a dozen fourteen-year-olds she knew who had gone to house parties. Mrs. Delahanty, at that, had shifted her ground. Fourteen might not be too young if the other girls were fourteen. But if the other girls were fifteen and sixteen and even, as in the case of that Perrotti girl, seventeen, Cress would be out of her depth, expected to know what she did not know, and interested in what didn't interest her; and she would hence have a miserable, disillusioning time.

To this Cress had replied that she saw the five house-party girls every day at school, that they were all interested in the same things (what these were she had not said) and that she was never uncomfortable or out of her depth with them. Mrs. Delahanty had then changed her tack. She had become very practical. Cress, with her fair skin and no one to look after her, would surely have one of her terrible cases of sunburn. And indigestion. Many a woman she knew traced her chronic indigestion to girlhood follies in eating. And where were these follies more practiced than at house parties? "Dill pickles! Potato chips! Cracker Jack!"

"Cracker Jack," Cress had echoed with real astonishment, "I've never tasted it. I never heard of anyone who did."

"You've heard of me," Mrs. Delahanty had replied shortly.

"Mother, I assure you Cracker Jack is no hazard," Cress had answered.

Sidetracked, Mrs. Delahanty had then retorted, "Hazard, Cress. I didn't say it was a hazard. I said . . ." But she had seen through the sidetracking technique. "Cracker Jack is beside the point. Conglomerations of food at odd hours."

"You forget Miss Bird," Cress had said. Miss Bird was to be their chaperone. She was an aunt of Maribeth Dufour's, whose idea the house party was.

"Oh yes," Mrs. Delahanty had replied. "The biology teacher."

"And biology is about food," Cress had said, arranging biology to fit her needs. "Miss Bird probably has lists of balanced meals already made out and ready for us to follow."

Mrs. Delahanty had left off talking about indigestion at that. "What I really worry about, Cress, is drowning. Scarcely a summer goes by without my reading of a drowning or two at a house party."

"Miss Bird is a wonderful swimmer. She is a little lame and can't go hiking or anything. So she swims."

"Like Byron," Mrs. Delahanty had said, unexpectedly. And then, in spite of the fact that Byron was surely the last person to hit on as a suitable chaperone for a girl's house party, she added, "I must say Miss Bird sounds like the perfect chaperone."

That was exactly the light in which Maribeth had presented her aunt. "Aunt Iris," she had assured the girls, "is practically a prefabricated chaperone. The minute she gets to the beach she will put on a kind of divided skirt outfit she has had since 1920 and which she has since shortened some, but not much. And she will sally forth with her specimen case to hunt marine specimens and we will scarcely ever see Aunt Iris again. She will, in fact, leave us perfectly free."

The house-party girls, when Maribeth had said this, had been eating lunch together in the high school cafeteria. Cornelia Samms, at whose parents' beach cottage the house party was to be held, had looked at Maribeth over a spoonful of trembling lime jello and asked, "Free for what, Maribeth?"

Everyone but poor Cornelia had known the answer to this question. They would be free for the word no one spoke. Cress had squirmed because of Corny's ignorance. And because Corny's question had demonstrated so perfectly why Cornelia was so lucky in possessing parents who owned beach and mountain cottages they were willing for Corny's friends to use. But Maribeth, without squirming

and with her famous wide-open, violet-eyed stare un-
clouded, had answered, "Oh, free for whatever you like,
Corny. Who am I to say what that is? Swimming in the
nude, maybe." She had suggested this in her off-hand,
flattering way, as if Corny were an unpredictable and daring scamp.

Corny, at that, had clasped the big unsuitable alligator
bag which she always carried to school to her matronly
bosom, as if Maribeth's suggestion had already undressed
her. "Oh, Maribeth," she had breathed, whistling a little,
as she did when excited, because there was a gap between
her two front teeth. "I wouldn't think of such a thing."

"It was just a suggestion, Cornelia. The point is, with
Aunt Iris for chaperone we'll be free. For whatever we
want." And she and all the girls except Corny had looked
at each other with understanding. What they'd be free for
was boys. That was the unsaid word and the whole point
of the house party as everyone except Corny well understood.

Cress, damp and cold where the sand touched her, dry
and cold where the wind blew across her, thought about
that freedom and the way she was using it. Yolande and
her boy friend were counting waves to see if every seventh
wave was, as people said, the biggest.

Listening, Cress had an idea about waves, which would
lead her quite naturally into the conversation: Wasn't the
big seventh wave a shepherd herding six small sheep ahead

of him? She took her arms from across her face, then put them back without speaking. After all Yolande *hadn't* introduced her.

Even after her mother had said that Cress could go to the house party she had kept asking about it. Yesterday morning, though that seemed years ago now, her mother had brought orange juice in to her, and had sat on her bed while she drank it.

"Just exactly who are these girls you are going with, Cress?" she had asked.

"Well, they are the school leaders," Cress had answered, a little uncertain as to where to start in her descriptions.

"Are they your friends?"

"Why, Mother! Of course they are. Maribeth—"

"Maribeth I know. Likewise Cornelia. And I've heard all about Yolande I care to. But who is this Mavis Avis?"

"Mavis Davis," Cress had corrected her mother. "And her sister, Avis Davis."

"Mavis and Avis!" Mrs. Delahanty had repeated. "You wouldn't think parents could do that to children they loved."

Privately, Cress believed that parents had a blind spot about their children's names. She had heard a few remarks herself about the unsuitability of Crescent. But all she had said was, "But Mother, they're twins, identical twins. They dress exactly alike, except for jeweled initial pins. That's so they can tell themselves apart. It doesn't matter to anyone else, since they're exactly the same. Mavis and Avis Davis! Those names really mesmerize me."

"I can see they do," Mrs. Delahanty had agreed.

Cress had defended herself. "It's not *just* their names. They're the school yell leaders. They've trained themselves to talk in absolute unison like Jack Benny's Sportsmen. It's terrifically uncanny."

Mrs. Delahanty had made a sound in her throat. "In private conversation, you mean they do that?"

Cress had nodded with pride. "How can you stand them, Cress? Talking together that way?" her mother had asked.

Actually, although Cress had not known it yesterday morning, when answering her mother's questions, the twins, when separated from their official duties as yell leaders and drum majorettes, had almost nothing to say. Cress slept with Mavis. Aunt Iris had separated the twins because she believed it would help develop independence in them. Last night's separation had not helped Mavis much, Cress thought, since Mavis had spoken only twice and had both times said the same thing. "That goes double for me." Though this was, perhaps, an advance, since when together they stood like statuary in their identical dresses and stared out from under their identically cut black bangs with their gray duplicating eyes and once in a while, but not very often, said something in unison the way twin statues would, if wired to speak. Maribeth had declared when the house-party guest list was being planned that, with Mavis and Avis along, people at the beach couldn't

help noticing them. Cress had been unwise enough to re-
peat this to her mother.

"People?" Mrs. Delahanty had repeated. "People?"
For a minute the unsaid word of everybody's house party
was on the verge of being spoken. For what Mrs. Delahanty had almost said of course was "boys." "*Boys*," not
"people," would notice the house-party girls with the twins
along; and what the girls would be free for, with Aunt
Iris as chaperone, would be *boys*. *Boys* would see them
as they tossed their shining, newly shampooed hair in great
exaggerated arcs after they took off their bathing caps; and
boys would hear them when they ran back into the water,
shouting and splashing. And *boys* would see them again,
when they came out of the water and stood drying themselves with gestures slower and more deliberate than necessary in the slanting afternoon sun.

And they would not only be seen, they would see. They
would see the big athletes and the track stars and the football players and perhaps even the Southern California
Interscholastic Tennis Champion who lived at Balboa
Beach. They would notice out of the corners of their eyes
the showy handstands of these boys and their professional
stance on the surfboards, as they came racing shoreward
on the crests of the largest breakers. They would see the
non-athletes, too—the presidents of student bodies and
the commissioners of activities, the boys in flowered shorts
and horn-rimmed spectacles, who would organize softball
games and blow up rubber horses. They would also notice, or she would anyway, the boys of slighter build, quiet

boys, neither athletes nor executives, who swam as if they
liked the feel of water and picked up handfuls of sand
and watched it trickle between their fingers with the sunshine gilding it. And one of these boys, his black hair dried
in starfish points, and a sweater hung over his shoulders
to protect his sunburn, would be somebody's cousin or
brother's friend or ex-classmate; and he, after being introduced, and a little talk to everyone for politeness' sake,
would toss a small shell in her direction and say to her
alone, "Can *you* always tell when it's Sunday, because
there's a Sunday shine in the air?" Something really personal, and about which they two alone would have any
knowledge. And after that, a private world, like a great
bubble, would settle down over the two of them.

When Yolande's friend had come up out of the water,
Cress had thought for a minute that he was going to be this
boy of the Sunday shine and the private world. But now
he was leaving—without a shell, or even a word, tossed
to her.

Just before supper Cress had to listen, once more, to the
story of how this boy had come up out of the water to talk
to her and Yolande and how she, mum as an oyster, had
left to Yolande the whole burden of entertaining him.
The girls, with Aunt Iris, were in the solarium, a big glass-
walled room facing the sea.

Outside the water, which had been a dusty plum, was
changing back to morning's green; though there were
white caps now which made it look littered and untidy,

like the beach itself, with its forgotten towels and straggling bathers. The low sun shone through the thinned
top of the breakers, coloring them, as they broke, the pink
of a raspberry soda; the nastiest pink in the world, Cress
thought, waiting for the final, and by now familiar, line of
Yolande's story.

She looked away from the sea to the room. Aunt Iris
faced her at the other end of the big window, her head
inclined over an old copy of *Scientific American*, unaware,
it appeared, of anything but what she was reading. She
had changed from her khaki divided-skirt costume to a
soft rose-colored silk and she had pinned a rhinestone butterfly to her thick gray braids and tucked an embroidered
handkerchief under the edge of her belt so that the embroidered corner protruded festively, like a flower.

The twins, in T-shirts and short white pleated drum
majorette skirts, silently practiced a cheerleader routine
in the arch of the doorway, dip, dip, dip, leap. But their
faces, turned toward Yolande, reflected the meaning of
Yolande's words: what a crazy girl Cress is. Maribeth, on
the arm of Yolande's chair, was openly laughing. Only
Corny, in a white dress that made her look all the plumper,
appeared sympathetic, thinking, Cress believed, there except for the grace of God go I.

"This boy," Yolande went on, "was a complete and
absolute stranger to me. But after he left, do you know
what Cress said to me?"

They most certainly did. Yolande had told them at
least twice before, and Cress, seeing that she was going

to tell them once again, looked out at the sea and tried, stoically, to count waves. "After he left," Yolande said, her voice as shocked with disbelief as if she had never repeated Cress's words before, "she said, 'Yolande, why didn't you introduce your friend to me?' Can you really believe it?" she asked, hooting with laughter. "Anything so childish? Thinking I wouldn't talk to him if I didn't know him?"

Maribeth, holding her stomach to keep her laughs from shaking her too much, called across to Cress. "Oh, Cress, not really?"

Yolande saved Cress from answering. "Yes, yes, she really did. Honest, can you imagine anything so naive?"

Yolande and Maribeth laughed for a long time. The twins, landing in a semi-split after a leap, said together, "Rah, rah-rah. Fight 'em, fight 'em, fight 'em."

Cornelia, face down, pleated her full white skirt. Cress counted meager waves, seconds and thirds and fourths, it looked like, though far out in the greening, plum-colored water she saw a big one forming.

Aunt Iris put down the *Scientific American* and struggled in her slow heavy way up from her chair. Don't defend me, Cress thought, don't say what a good sweet girl I am and make them all hate me.

Aunt Iris didn't. All she said was, "I don't know about you girls, but I'm hungry." And she led them to the dining room.

After supper it was as if the girls had never avoided the word boys, as if the boy who had come up out of the sea had been a sign to them to talk and speculate. They had planned to go to a movie, but they went back to the solarium, instead, and there in the summery darkness, without bothering to turn on the lights, they began to wonder and to gossip. They perched on chair arms, cloudy, moth-like in their light flimsy dresses; or lay on the floor (the twins) immobile and, with their tunic skirts and long solid legs, looking now like Greek statuary fallen; though once in a while two legs, Avis' left and Mavis' right, were simultaneously lifted at right angles to their bodies, thus spoiling the statuary effect.

Cress sat on the hassock which Aunt Iris had used to support her lame leg (Aunt Iris herself had taken the *Scientific American* and gone to her room) and watched the green-silver phosphorescence which occasionally smoked at a wave's tip and, further out, the single bobbing red light of a boat moving slowly across the horizon. A couple went by on the sand below the solarium windows, singing "Fight On for Old U.C.," to which someone out of sight (a boy) yelled, "Give 'em the ax."

The talk was mostly Yolande's and Maribeth's, with questions now and then from Corny. They talked of what boys were like, *really*, and how they were different from girls, and what they liked in girls, *really*.

"Looks are not so important," Yolande said in her clear contralto, which sounded, Cress thought, like a large bell lightly rung. But it was easy for Yolande with her gypsy princess face to belittle looks.

Maribeth said, "I know. Look at Amanda Peters."

"She's got a wonderful figure," Corny said mournfully. Corny hadn't any figure at all, not even a bad one.

Cress, hoping a plain fact couldn't be considered naive, said, "Mindy Jackson hasn't got either." And everyone knew Mindy was the most popular girl-with-boys in school.

Mavis, speaking by herself (perhaps Aunt Iris' theory about separation and independence was right) said, "It's a complete mystery."

Yolande corrected her. "It's chemistry," she said, in a dreamy voice, "pure chemistry."

Maribeth agreed. "Either you have it, or you don't."

"Is it all settled when you're born?" Corny asked, as if her fate hung in the balance.

"I expect so, Corny," Yolande answered cheerfully, giving her long earrings a clink, like an echo to the bell of her voice. "Some girls have the kind of chemistry only one boy reacts to. Or maybe two. Mindy Jackson has universal chemistry."

"What happens if a girl with ten per cent chemistry meets a boy with one hundred per cent chemistry?" Corny wanted to know.

"She's lucky," Yolande said promptly.

"Are there many boys like that?" Cress asked.

"No, thank goodness," Maribeth said.

The last of day was now gone but there was enough light from stars or moon, or reflected off the sea to show Yolande's slow white smile.

"I wouldn't say that, Maribeth," she said. Then before

Maribeth, or anyone else could answer, she broke the spell
by flicking on the lamp at her elbow. "It's only eight-
thirty," she said. "Let's go to the second show."

They came home from the show, an old Alan Ladd
movie, with their eyes full of rippling muscles and smoking guns.

"Anybody sleepy?" Yolande asked. No one was.

"Anyone hungry?" Maribeth wanted to know. Everyone was. Cress stirred up her own special concoction called
cocoa-mud: cocoa and sugar with just enough cream to
make it spreadable. They ate it on thick slices of heavily
buttered French bread and washed it down with Coca-
Cola. It was very invigorating and after eating everyone
felt peppy.

The twins led them in a drum-majorette routine. Cress
did handstands. Yolande sang a French song. They had a
contest to see who could drink a whole coke without taking
a breath. They had another contest to see who, with a
bottle of coke shaken to the exploding point, could hit the
most distant target.

At midnight, Aunt Iris, in a flowered challis dressing
gown, stepped into the hall that opened into the kitchen
and said, "Save something for tomorrow, girls."

In their own room Cress and Mavis sat on their twin
Hollywood beds. Cress felt boiling with life, as if there
were more blood in her veins than her veins could hold,
and more veins in her body than her body could contain.
She felt, as she sometimes did when reading a noble book,

as if the earth and its glories were about to be spread
before her and their deepest meanings made clear. Only
tonight, the book was her life, not just the imaginings of
some writer, and somewhere, outside this room, a new page
was waiting to be turned.

Outside was the summer night and the stars with their
jabbing lights and the sea, whose booming she felt as a
pulse inside her head rather than as sound. And only
seven blocks away dance bands were playing and cars were
drawing up to the curb, laden with people for whom the
night was just beginning. She could see it all very clearly.
The skin was tight across her cheekbones, and her lips felt
strong and curling, simply with the excitement of being
alive. There was no use trying to tell from Mavis' expression *what* she felt, but at least she didn't look sleepy.

Cress jumped off her twin Hollywood bed and went
and stood over Mavis. "Oh, Mavis," she implored, "let's
do something. Let's not just sit here moldering. Let's
. . ." But she didn't know what let's do. Only let's get
up, move, go outside, stay awake, give the world and the
night a chance.

But Mavis knew. Perhaps she was not a talker but she
knew what to *do*. "Let's go get the Samms' boat," she
said, "and row on the bay."

"Yes," Cress said. "Oh yes. That will be perfect. Let's
row till sunup."

The Samms kept a rowboat tied up alongside their big
cabin cruiser, a little white rowboat named "Cornelia"

and Cress felt disloyal to Corny, slipping out of the house without a word to her to row in a boat which was her namesake. But Corny was no rower and Mavis was.

With Mavis rowing by her side, they cut silently through the jagged, multi-colored spears of light which were reflected onto the water from the pier where the dance band played. They rowed in time to the music— every other beat was just right. There were many boats out, but no one else, it was obvious, was out simply to row, to be abroad in the night, exposed to starshine and supported by water. Simply to row? To look at the stars? Oh no! That was not true and Cress knew it.

They were rowing toward someone, rowing toward a voice, a meeting on the water, toward the boy who would present the lovely shell and speak the secret words about the Sunday shine, the boy who would make the page turn and the meaning clear, as in the noblest book, here in the summer night, afloat on the dark reflecting water. As soon as she had admitted this, it was time to stop rowing; she felt sleepy and tired. What did she expect? Magic? A barge appearing out of darkness like that which bore the dying King Arthur away? An arm from the water clothed in white samite?

But with the "Cornelia" tied up once more, and someone (the dance band had gone home) playing a piano, sitting down in front of it and repeating a phrase as a radio player never did, and with the tide lifting the boats on the bay in a ceaseless sickle-shaped swing, leaving seemed ignoble. Or at least undaring. (And were they

the same?) Was she giving up her search too easily? Had
this been a test and was the pattern of her life being decided this minute? Oh come, knowledge and beauty. She
asked it of the night and of the water, extending her arms
upward and curling her toes earthward in her brown and
white saddle shoes. "Come, knowledge and beauty," she
said aloud.

Mavis perhaps did not understand her. Or perhaps did,
and offered the best she had. Somewhere, from in or under her white drum-majorette kilt, she brought up a
package of cigarettes, lit one for herself, then handed
package and matches to Cress. It was not the first cigarette
Cress had ever had between her lips, nor the first puff she
had ever taken. But she had never before taken more than
one puff, and that only in front of a mirror, for the sake
of what she saw there. Tonight smoking seemed, clearly,
the thing to do. She walked homeward with Mavis, past
the still lit bars and cafés and pool halls, trying to imitate
Mavis' nonchalance. It was beyond her, though; she could
manage neither the down-drooping cigarette, nor Mavis'
practiced majorette flip of her skirt.

However short she came of Mavis, she did not come
short enough to completely offset the effect of Mavis'
black bangs, brown legs and sashaying white pleats. Maribeth had been more than right. People noticed the twins,
even when separated; and her mother had been right, the
name for people was boys. Boys looked and spoke as they
went past and at the corner where they turned right, two
boys who had been watching them as they came down the

street turned right with them, and falling in behind them, kept pace with them. "Aren't you two girls out pretty late?" they asked.

They were kids, Cress saw, sixteen or seventeen, and they did not attempt to catch up with them and she didn't feel anything but uncomfortable until, as they were leaving the lights of the business district, three more boys joined the queue. Then she was frightened. Mavis was too; she could tell by Mavis' grip on her arm and the increased speed of her walking. And there were two more blocks before they would reach home, blocks shadowed by palm and jacaranda trees and misted with the morning fog already drifting in off the ocean.

Mavis, without turning her head, whispered, "Let's run."

"No," Cress whispered back. What was the sense of that? The boys could surely run faster than they could, and once running was started, all pretense that the boys just happened to be going their way would be lost. Though there was no denying that they were all walking faster and faster; nor that she couldn't tell the sound of her heart, it was beating so hard, from the sound of the surf.

And all the time the boys were calling to them, asking their names, where they went to school, what track team they were training for. "What's your best time for the 440, girls?" they asked. "What's that thing you're wearing for a skirt?" they called to Mavis. And, to Cress, "Hey, sweater girl, turn around." It was worse than frightening, it was cheap, and Cress's face burned.

"What you looking for, girls, that we ain't got?" they called, and Cress thought how stupid she had been, lifting her arms over the water, asking for beauty and knowledge —when this was the answer, this cheapness and humiliation. The boys were gaining on them, coming closer and closer, and one of the boys used a word whose meaning she didn't know but whose sound was ugly.

In the minute before they would have reached the Samms' house, they were suddenly surrounded. The boys' tone was still joking. One of them, an unlit cigarette in his mouth, said: "Give us a light, will you, girls?" But in spite of the joke, the boys stood in that unyielding circle, close about Cress and Mavis.

Cress, trembling, in a voice that scarcely emerged from her dry throat, said, and was hardly aware of what she said: "Is *that* all you want?"

These words, somehow, gave immediate pause to the joking. Miraculously the circle of boys opened, and the two girls walked through the gate and into the Samms' yard. Once inside the yard, and the gate slammed behind them, they began to run.

Neither spoke until they reached their own room and had that door closed behind them, too. Then Mavis, not in the least winded by the sprinting, said: "I don't want to sleep in the same room with you any more, Cress Delahanty." And having said that, she calmly left. In a few minutes she returned with Avis. "I'm going to sleep with my own twin," she told Cress. "You go on down to Corny's room."

"Mavis," Cress asked, "what's the matter?"

"You know," Mavis said, as she and Avis moved with their duplicating steps across the floor.

Cress, pajamas in hand, went down to Corny's room. There Corny, her round face heavy with doubt, looked at her suspiciously. Cress apologized. "I'm sorry to be disturbing you, Corny. But the twins got homesick for each other."

"No," Corny said. "It wasn't homesickness for each other. It was disgust for you."

"Me?" Cress asked.

"What you said to those boys," Corny explained. "What you asked them."

Cress moved up to the bed and in real amazement said, "But, Corny . . ." Corny cut her short. "And you've been smoking, too. You really reek, Cress. I don't blame Mavis for not wanting to sleep with you. I don't want to either. I don't think Mother would like me to, in fact."

"Mavis smoked too," Cress said, feeling like a tattle-tale.

"She doesn't *reek*," Corny persisted, turning away from her with finality.

Rejection by Corny, who wanted everyone, even stray dogs, to love her, was the final humiliation. Cress, without a further word, went out to the living room. She could sleep on the sofa and in the morning she would hitch-hike home. But before she had undone a button Aunt Iris, still in her flowered dressing gown and with butterfly pin

still aloft, though now somewhat askew, came to the doorway. "What is all this uproar about?" she asked.

"Corny doesn't want to sleep with me," Cress said.

"Why?" Aunt Iris asked.

"She says I reek."

Aunt Iris was beside her now, sniffing. "Reek?" she
asked. "What of?"

"Tobacco," Cress said. "Mavis and I went rowing and
on the way home we smoked."

"I thought Mavis was the one you were sleeping with
anyway, not Corny," Aunt Iris said.

"Mavis doesn't want to sleep with me either," Cress
admitted.

"Why?" Aunt Iris asked. "She reeks too, doesn't she?"

"Mavis doesn't mind the tobacco. What she doesn't like
is something I said. Anyway, that's what she says."

"To her?"

"No. To some boys."

"What did you say?" Aunt Iris asked.

Cress told her. Aunt Iris said not a word but with face
averted took the rhinestone butterfly from her braids and
examined it closely. "One stone missing," she said finally,
replacing the butterfly more securely. "You come on down
to my room," she told Cress, "and sleep with me. I reek
too."

It was a fact. Aunt Iris' room was hazed with smoke.
"During the war," Aunt Iris said, "when cigarettes were
hard to get, I smoked a corncob pipe. I got to like it, but

in a girls' school I had to keep my door locked for fear of shocking someone."

Cress stared at Aunt Iris in astonishment. The idea of Aunt Iris shocking, instead of being shocked, was too great a reversal for her to comprehend so suddenly. Ignoring the image of Aunt Iris with a pipe, she said, "I'm sorry I waked you," which was the truth and was, besides, all she could think of to say at the minute.

"I hadn't gone to bed yet," Aunt Iris told her. "I was working, then listening to music, then working again." She waved her hand toward two card tables, placed side by side and holding what Cress thought of as "chemistry equipment"—objects, anyway, having to do with a laboratory—microscope, shallow dishes, an aquarium. But the room was filled with many things; books, magazines, a portable phonograph—it looked like a place where a person was living, not empty and bare as the girls' rooms were, places where they were only waiting.

Aunt Iris opened a window, using a magazine to fan out some of the smoke. Then, leaning from the window, she said: "I should've done this earlier. It's a beautiful balmy night. Smell the iodine and salt and the bitter-sweet of the kelp." She extended her arms into the night air and the big sleeves fell away from them and Cress saw that, while round and heavy, they were also firm and muscular; saw that Aunt Iris with her broad shoulders and deep bosom, her full lips and straight but fleshy nose, was like a Roman matron. "There," Aunt Iris said, pointing, "is Vega. Clear, inscrutable, light years distant, reflected, since first its burning reached us, in how many billion billion eyes, human and inhuman?" Aunt Iris was moving her big strong arms in the air outside the windows now, rotating them as if she were bathing them in the night's freshness.

She turned from the window. "I tell you what we both need, Cress, since we both reek. A little dip. Ten minutes only. We'll sleep better for it."

Cress said, "My suit's down in the twins' room."

"Suit?" Aunt Iris asked. "What do you need a suit for at this hour of the night?"

Cress didn't know. So she said nothing. "Here," Aunt Iris said, "you can wear this to the water." It was a smock, Cress guessed, or a laboratory coat of the kind doctors wore. She undressed in silence, modestly turned away from Aunt Iris who, when she faced about, had on a white toweling robe.

The air outside was sweet and fresh, even a little sharp. Cress had to slow her steps for Aunt Iris, whose lameness gave her a clumsy laborious gait.

"I never reconcile myself to this," Aunt Iris said, slapping her crippled leg, "never, never."

Cress, trying to equal Aunt Iris' matter-of-factness, asked, "Was it that way—from the beginning?"

"Do you mean was I born with it? No. No. I got this in a most unlikely way, in a cyclone. When I was nineteen. At a dance in a schoolhouse in Kansas. I was the teacher," she said, turning to speak over her shoulder and raising her voice to be heard above the surf. "In a way I was lucky that night, in a way I wasn't. Five people were killed. One of them was the boy I was going to marry that summer. That was my life's bad luck."

They were at the water's edge now and Aunt Iris took off her white robe and threw it back up the beach and stood before Cress, a large indistinct column in the darkness of the night.

"You couldn't ever love anyone else?" Cress asked, trying to take in the whole of Aunt Iris' life from that long-ago night in Kansas to this moment on the edge of the Pacific.

"Oh yes," Aunt Iris shouted, "I could indeed. But not any of those who were able themselves to love a lame woman." She had stopped to say these words. Now she began to wade slowly out in the water.

Cress threw off her own covering and walked into the water, milky warm after the night air. Ahead of her, ungainly, but steadfast in front of the deepening breakers, was Aunt Iris. "Would you like to go out with me tomorrow?" she called back. "These rock pools here are regular mines for algae."

Hunting algae with Aunt Iris had been the last thing Cress had ever imagined doing on a house party. The last thing she had imagined a house party could be *for*. But as the warm water rose from knee to thigh to waist, and then went sliding shoreward past her, she did not seem to have lost, either the imagined house party, or the imagined boy with the shell and the words about the Sunday shine. She caught up handfuls of water and dashed them across her chest and face.

Aunt Iris was waiting for her and Cress called above the surf, "Oh yes, I do want to go. Please may I?"

Aunt Iris, without answering, faced the open sea again and motioning with one big arm for Cress to follow, dived under the wall of the comber toppling above her. Cress followed, diving less cleanly; but she came up out of the smother in open water, only a little breathless, and swam easily in Aunt Iris' wake.

Spring

As soon as Cress left the breakfast table to catch the school bus, Mrs. Delahanty told her husband what she had done.

"I'm not going to say a word to Cress about it until the night before," she concluded. "If I do she'll find reasons for backing out. She's got a half-dozen acts she can do perfectly. Practice would just make her stiff and nervous. I'll tell her the night before, at the earliest, that I've given my word she'll appear. She won't like it but in the long run it will be for her own good." Mrs. Delahanty's uncertainty about what she had done made her unusually positive in her manner. "Don't you think so, John?" she asked, when her husband said nothing.

Mr. Delahanty poured the last of the waffle batter onto the iron and put down the lid. Then he took a leisurely drink of coffee. He wasn't sure that he *did* think so. "I don't know, Gertrude," he said finally; then, as he saw his wife believed he was simply being evasive, he added, "Honestly, I don't."

"You think it's our duty to encourage Cress to develop her talents, don't you?"

239

"Some of them, I guess."

"Your waffle's burning, John," Mrs. Delahanty said, without much sorrow in her voice.

Mr. Delahanty took it out, chocolate-colored and smoking. "Our trouble, Cress's too probably, is that she's an only child."

Mrs. Delahanty's face, which had been so animated when she spoke of her plans for Cress, became sad. Mr. Delahanty reassured her. "I'm just evading the issue, Gertrude."

"You do agree, don't you," she asked, "that this is an improvement over last winter?" She indicated the improvements with head and hand: the blinds rolled to the tops of the windows; the tie-back curtains really tied back so that the glassed-in end of the kitchen where they were eating was filled with April sunshine. Almost filled, it seemed, with orange trees too, for the orchard was so close that a long arm could reach out from the breakfast table and pick fruit or blossoms. It was blossoms, now; the Valencias wouldn't be ripe until July; blossoms and mocking birds and towhees. Every morning lately a towhee had tried to fly through the glass of the windows to sample the French toast and scrambled eggs. For there was, once again, French toast and scrambled eggs; and waffles and cream gravy and strawberry preserves. The health foods had gone with the semi-darkness.

Mr. Delahanty, setting his waffle afloat in syrup, said, "It's a great improvement. No comparison between now and last winter."

Mrs. Delahanty nodded. "I can't remember a more miserable winter."

"Tragedy, tragedy all the way," Mr. Delahanty agreed.

"And no real cause for tragedy. That's what makes it so sad. No sickness. No death."

Without attempting to follow this line of reasoning, Mr. Delahanty said, "At fourteen you don't need sickness or death for tragedy."

The darkness, or semi-darkness, for instance, in which they had lived out the winter: at first he had believed it to be accidental. He would come into the house, find the blinds all half down and go about systematically raising them. "Living like owls," he would say to Cress, cheerfully, as if he himself were the one responsible for the gloom. "Getting to the place my eyes water every time I step outside," he'd say as he set the blinds to flying upward.

If Cress had made any reply to these sallies, he couldn't remember them. His remembrance was that she had said nothing. But when he re-entered a room there, once more, would be the pulled blinds, the cave-dweller gloom. Finally he had remarked on it. "What's the big idea, Cress? All this darkness?"

Cress had given him a long reproachful look. "Is it necessary, Father, to tell you in so many words? Can't you see for yourself? Without my crying it from the housetops?"

"I'm still in the dark, Cress," he had said, pleased at the time with the pun.

Cress, at that, had raised every curtain and then in the

clear light of the December afternoon had lifted her face for his inspection. "Need I say any more?"

"I guess you'll have to, Cress," he had told her, still uncertain as to what she was driving at.

Then with a movement both tragic and courageous, like a martyr offering her neck to the ax, she had said, "Look at my complexion, Father."

He had looked, carefully. And seeing a little unevenness, a little redness possibly, had replied honestly, "Well, in this light, Cress . . ." But Cress had not let him finish. "Then it is visible. Oh I just hate this light. Why do people want to live in a glare? Where everything ugly is so plain. When I grow up I'm going to have soft, soft lights everywhere."

"Now, Cress," he had begun, reasonably, "you know people aren't bats. And at your age a pimple or t—"

Cress had not let him finish. She had put her hands over her face and made sounds, halfway between sorrow and nausea. When these had stopped she said in a whisper, "I wouldn't say such a disgusting word to an animal—let alone my own daughter."

Mr. Delahanty had tried to reassure her. "I wouldn't have said a word—not of any kind, except you insisted and only then . . ."

Cress had taken down her hands. "It *is* perfectly visible then," she asked, bleakly, "to the naked eye?"

"I don't know that it's perfectly visible, but in this light I can see, now that my attention is called to it"—he had searched for an acceptable word—"a bump or—"

"Bump?" Cress had whispered. "Bump? It's more than a spot then?"

He had given up, at that, hunting the right word. "Cress, you're being silly. There isn't a man or woman alive who hasn't had complexion trouble at your age."

She had contradicted him fiercely. "Oh yes there are. Did you ever read *Laddie?*"

He thought he had. "A book about a collie? By Albert Payson Terhune?"

"Oh no. This book is about a young man and it's by Gene Stratton Porter. It's a beautiful book and Laddie is my ideal. Laddie's blood stream was so pure and his living so vivid that the bloom on his coffee and roses skin had never once been marred by the slightest flaw. That's almost the exact words. I didn't try to memorize them but I never look at myself without thinking of them. His blood stream so pure, his living so vivid! Isn't that beautiful! And look at me. Oh it's disgusting."

Out of complete inability to cope with this heartbreak and unreason Mr. Delahanty had pulled down with great finality the curtains Cress had raised for his examination of her complexion. "Cress," he had said, "if it makes you feel better to have things a little gloomy I don't see why not. We've had blazing sunlight in this house for fifteen years. If you want a little darkness now it's your turn to call the trick."

So, in semi-darkness and eating sparsely, they had lived through the winter. The sparse diet was not the result of Cress's desire for a flawless complexion—but for vivid

living, a revolt against the grossness of the world. Anna
Pavlova, Cress said, weighed ninety-two pounds. Thomas
A. Edison ate four water biscuits for lunch. So what were
they, the Delahantys, doing eating great pots of Spanish
rice and platters of Swiss steak and pans of Lazy-Daisy
coffee cake? And weighing one hundred and eighty-two,
one hundred and thirty-five, and one hundred and seventeen pounds respectively? They, who were not geniuses
or dancers or inventors or artists?

The least they could do was to eat like a genius, wasn't
it? Wasn't it? There was no loving answer to this insane
logic so they, without hope of anything but losing a pound
or two, lived plain, at least at the table (away from the
table Mr. Delahanty had an unplain bite or two) and
tried to think high. Hominy grits with canned apricots for
dessert. It was pallid fare in the midst of the semi-darkness. Mr. Delahanty had begun to feel—if not like Edison—at least like Byrd at the South Pole. But he had not
Byrd's sustaining knowledge of emerging eventually into
sunlight, full rations, and with the plaudits of an admiring
and sympathetic public for his ordeal. And though he did
it all, if not gladly, at least resignedly, for Cress's sake,
Cress seemed none the happier for it. Her complexion
continued to be flawed and her living un-vivid. She went
to a party and was the only girl there in a sweater, a miserable conspicuous person. She made a speech in assembly
welcoming a delegation from a neighboring high school
and pronounced the word hospitable with the accent on
the second syllable. She had volunteered a piece of mis-

taken information in her English class, insisting that a poem by T. S. Eliot had been written by Edwin Arlington Robinson. She was not elected, as she had expected to be, editor of her year book. She read Mrs. Gaskell's *Life of Charlotte Brontë* and wondered if, after what the Brontës had suffered, anyone had a right to be happy.

Then, in the midst of all these misfortunes, the California winter rains still falling, grossness still abroad in the world, her complexion flawed and her weight stationary at one hundred and fourteen, she had come home from school one afternoon to send every blind flying to the top of the window and to ask for French-fried shrimps and chocolate pudding for dinner. And she had eaten them with no thought, as far as Mr. Delahanty could see, of Anna Pavlova, Thomas A. Edison, or Laddie. And after dinner she had been funny, consciously, clownishly, ridiculously funny. As an entertainer is. They had laughed, they couldn't help themselves. But they had been troubled. Back of the funniness there had been tensity, a suggestion of the clown's conscious assumption of a mask, beneath which a life unguessed, and possibly quite contradictory to the side-splitting façade, existed.

"Why this sudden change, Cress?" her father had asked.

"Change?" Cress echoed, as if feasting, bright lights, and jollity had been their winter's routine.

"All this jollity? All these non-water biscuits?"

"Life," Cress had answered, quoting again but not from Gene Stratton Porter, "is a tragedy for those who feel and a comedy for those who think."

And there, for all the further information given them, the matter rested. And if thinking meant comedy, then Cress had become a thinker, for there was no let-up in the comedy. Dinners were mirthful and breakfasts, with the spring sunlight putting a green-gold dazzle across the white tablecloth, were merry. The fun had not only continued through March and into April but it had developed as it continued. It was a little like living with a cross between Martha Graham and Groucho Marx: dancing with a wisecrack.

"The trouble is," Mrs. Delahanty confessed to her husband as she took the last bite of his syrup-logged waffle, "that I don't know what to call it."

"Call what?"

"Cress's act."

"Act" was a more formal word than Mr. Delahanty had himself ever applied to what Cress did. "Take-offs" had been his own name for these—whatever they were—imitations or dances or pantomimes or caricatures. But "take-off," he supposed, was too general a phrase for the talent committee. And though he did not wholly approve of what his wife was doing, still his mind engaged itself automatically with the verbal problem she had posed. "What would you think of 'Caricatures in Motion,'" he asked, "for a title?" She thought it would be fine; serious, unusual, and professional.

Mr. Delahanty, since his wife spoke of the matter no more, let it drop from his own mind. Spring vacation came and Cress's acts, while they continued, no longer struck him as a problem. On Tuesday evening of vacation week Cress entertained them after dinner with one of her best take-offs to date: the girl at a dance, who is a wall-flower and tries to hide the fact that she is dying with a broken heart by an excess of responsive smiles and clapping. It was very funny; also very sad, as the best comedy is. Mr. Delahanty laughed until he cried. At least there were tears on his cheeks when Cress finished and wandered off into the living room leaving her father and mother to savor second pieces of the still unaccustomed pleasures of pecan pie and whipped cream. Mr. Delahanty's savoring was arrested in mid-bite by Cress's return to the dining room, evening paper in hand.

"What is this?" she demanded.

"What is what, Cress?" Mrs. Delahanty asked, with a quaver of guilt in her voice which Mr. Delahanty with some pity recognized.

"List of Entrants for Talent Parade," Cress read. "The following individuals will participate in the Chamber of Commerce's Fifth Annual Talent Parade on Wednesday, April 7th. The Talent Parade has come to be anticipated, not only by the citizens of Tenant, but by residents of our sister cities. The Chamber of Commerce points with pride to the fact that their annual talent search has resulted in the discovery of such figures in the local entertainment fields as Deborah Dukes, xylophonist at the China Barn, and Billy Ryan, well-known tap dancer at many lodge meetings and community affairs. Wednesday's list of entrants includes the following performers, some already favorably known to followers of the arts in Tenant. 1. Trained Duck—Judith Connors. 2. Unicycle Act—Barry Zamalt. 3. The Topsborough Twins in Two-Ettes. 4. Moaning Low—Louella Enfield. 5. Charley and his Clarinet—Charles Mayberry. 6. Whistling Sam—Sam Harrison. 7. Caricatures in Motion—Crescent Delahanty." Letting the paper drop Cress asked, very distantly and coldly, "What are 'Caricatures in Motion'?" She said the three words, "Caricatures in Motion" as if they were some unknown but nasty-sounding dish on a menu. Mr. Delahanty left this question to his wife. She said, " 'Caricatures in Motion' was your father's idea for a title, Cress."

"Title for what?" Cress asked.

"What you just did. That girl at the dance."

"Oh," Cress said. "Why is *my* name on that list?"

"Because," Mrs. Delahanty told her, "I entered it. Because you have talent and I wanted other people to be able to enjoy what you can do. And you might win a prize."

"I don't want to win a prize. I hate prizes."

Mr. Delahanty, in spite of the fact that he'd had serious misgivings all along about this talent parade found himself, to his surprise, defending his wife. "Cress, without a push from us you would never have entered this, would you? You'd have found excuses."

"Yes," Cress said. "I would have."

"Oh, Cress," Mrs. Delahanty said, "if you really hate it, you don't have to do it. That list isn't legal or binding. Just refuse, just don't go."

"No," Cress said, "if you have given your word I'll do it." She stooped and picked up the newspaper, folded it carefully, then went to her room.

Mrs. Delahanty pushed her pecan pie aside. "Oh John," she said, "why did you let me?"

Mr. Delahanty finished his pie, but the responsibility thus handed him weighed heavily. The days of gloom and water biscuits seemed uncomplicated by contrast.

Two days later at ten o'clock Mr. and Mrs. Delahanty, along with five or six hundred other citizens of Tenant, stood on Jacaranda Street waiting for the Talent Parade to pass by.

"Can you see Cress?" Mrs. Delahanty asked. "She ought to be easy to see in that outfit she's got on."

"Not yet," Mr. Delahanty answered.

"Try to pick her out. I don't want to miss her. I want to wave. I want to—" She didn't finish her sentence but she didn't have to. Mr. Delahanty knew what she meant. She wanted to ask forgiveness, to make amends, to say, It was pride in you made me do it, Cress. It was love. Mr. Delahanty knew this because it was what he wanted to say, too.

The Chamber of Commerce had chosen Wednesday of Easter Week for the affair so that school children could participate. This choice had showed considerable confidence in the weather, even for a Chamber of Commerce, for early April can be cold and rainy in Southern California. But the Chamber's faith had been rewarded with a day for which even the announcer's superlatives were not excessive. "Brilliant sunshine," he was saying, "dazzling skies," "exotic blossoms," and it was all literally true. There was not a cloud, a breath of chill, or a single hibiscus or Paul scarlet with any apparent touch of blight or bite of earwig. Bands went by, drum majorettes spun and rotated like tops, batons flashed, loudspeakers mounted on floats proclaimed the virtues of a variety of products.

"I didn't know it would be like this," Mrs. Delahanty shouted. She had to shout to be heard above the V.F.W. band which was passing in front of them at that minute.

"What did you expect?" Mr. Delahanty shouted back.

"Dignity. Some dignity, anyway. Not so many automobiles advertising things. Not so many animals."

A boy of twelve or thirteen with a dog of about the same age went by. The dog was mustard-colored and trotted sidewise like a coyote. The boy's hair was crisscrossed in so intricate a pattern of uncombed strands that he appeared to be wearing a cap of basket-weave straw. Behind the boy an old man, a juggler, of all things, kept three red balls continuously mounting, flowing upward from his yellow hands like spray from an ancient fountain.

"Jugglers," Mrs. Delahanty shouted. "Ducks, dogs. Cress will be humiliated."

"It's no parade of simon-pure artists, that's a fact," Mr. Delahanty agreed.

It was also a fact that talent parade was beginning to look to him like some representative selection of mid-twentieth century humans, animals and artifacts being marched off to a time capsule for preservation for posterity. He began to feel like the father of a sacrificial victim, as if Cress were some Aztec maiden about to have her heart torn from her living body for the good of her tribe. And what were Cress's "take-offs" anyway but exposures of her heart? And why had he been so willing—or at least willing—for that exposure to take place? The anticipated praise? "This talented young lady, your daughter?" Cress's well-being? That one talent which is death to hide? Was being funny Cress's one talent? And why, at her age, had she developed a talent like that, anyway? The last resort of unhappy middle-aged men—a settling for the second best after the best is lost. A girl's dream wasn't ever of making Prince Charming *laugh*, was it? Cinderella didn't oblige at the ball with a caricature in motion, did she? Not after she saw that the crystal slipper was for her, anyway. But if you had no confidence? Well, you did something, you didn't give up. Not right away at least. Not if the old juggler was any sign. Sorrow at home and the curtains pulled was perhaps a better answer for a girl than this public merriment.

Mrs. Delahanty joggled him out of his abstractions. "There she is, John. Wave."

She was almost abreast of them before he saw her— dressed in some absurd costume, a smock or a shirt; a clear yellow with a brown sash which held the fullness of the material close to her tall, big-boned body. He waved eagerly but there was no response. Hadn't she seen him? Or was she already lost in anticipation of her take-off? Mrs. Delahanty waved and called, but Cress marched

straight on, a kind of self-conscious young Lady Godiva
in spite of her being thoroughly clothed. Behind her the
line of the talented was as long as that in front of her.
Mr. and Mrs. Delahanty marveled at its length. They
had had no idea of the amount of talent in Tenant. As
noon approached the sun became warmer and the last
marchers were pink-faced and warm, many of them carrying their coats. The announcer began to suggest that the
onlookers make their way to the bandstand in McHenry
Park where the performances were to take place. Mr. and
Mrs. Delahanty needed no urging. They wanted to be
there early in case Cress was among the first on the
program: and first or not they wanted to be where they
could see well.

They were charitable about the acts they saw while
waiting for Cress, though after a while Mrs. Delahanty
.said, "I don't know why *I* didn't enter." They had to admit, however, that the boy with the basket-weave hair
had a talented dog. The boy rolled through a series of
hoops and the dog, as the boy did this, leaped over him,
a kind of canine shadow projected upward instead of
downward. Mr. and Mrs. Delahanty applauded this spon-
taneously and a man next to them in a flowered seersucker
shirt said, "That's my boy." As the clapping continued,
he stopped. "No use overdoing it," he told the Delahantys. "There's plenty of others waiting for their chance.
You represented here?" he asked, tapping his program as
the applause died down.

Mr. Delahanty indicated Cress's name on the program. "Our daughter," he said.

"Glad to make your acquaintance, Mr. Delahanty. My name's Andrews. 'Caricatures in Motion,' eh? Sounds interesting. Just what are they?"

Mr. Delahanty went back to the phrase which he had supposed the Chamber of Commerce would not consider snappy enough, but which he now wished they had used, "take-offs." "They're take-offs, I guess."

"Take-offs? On what?"

"Well, various things. She's got a number of them. Ladies at bargain counters. People making speeches. Things like that."

"Funny, are they?" Andrews asked.

"We think so," Mr. Delahanty said. "Real funny."

But when Cress came out in her odd bag of a costume, so tacky after the sopranos in their beads and scarves and the tap dancers in their satin shorts, she was not funny at all. She was pitiful.

"What is this a take-off *on?*" Mr. Andrews asked in a polite but puzzled tone after watching for a minute or two.

"I'm as much at sea as you are," Mr. Delahanty said. "I never saw this before." And he was still at sea minutes later.

"Peculiar thing," Mr. Andrews remarked. "Maybe too deep for me. I can see the motion but I miss the caricature. I don't get what it's about."

Neither did Mr. Delahanty. But he kept his mouth

closed. If he didn't he felt he might cry. Whatever Cress's
bounding about up there was supposed to convey, it wasn't
funny. It wasn't entertaining in any other way either.
It was embarrassing, like watching the fumblings of a
lame man or a blind woman. Oh God, Mr. Delahanty
asked, let her get down from there before they start
laughing at her. They didn't do that. There was something too confiding and open about this big serious girl,
trying so hard to say something, do something—they
didn't know what, and failing. But they could not watch
her, it was too painful; they turned aside, they whispered
to each other; or in the beginning they whispered. Finally
they simply talked, relieved to pretend that what was hap-
pening up there on the bandstand was invisible. Except
for Mr. Andrews, the Andrews boy who had joined his
father, and Mr. and Mrs. Delahanty, Cress might as well
have been alone. Mr. Andrews studied the performance
seriously as if by concentration he could unravel some
meaning. But even he gave up.

"Your girl would be wise to call a halt about now."

Wise or not, Cress called a halt and the onlookers,
happy to be spared further pain, clapped enthusiastically.
Cress had, before the clapping began, given the crowd a
happy, confiding look, a refreshed look as if, though she
had traveled alone, she had arrived some place. She was
red-faced from all her leaping and prancing and her
short tow-colored hair stood up in points like the nimbus
around a child's drawing of the sun. Now, in response to

the applause, she made a happy, confiding bow, still child enough, it appeared, to believe that virtue's reward is love and appreciation.

Cress was at the car talking with Edwin when they got to the parking lot. Seeing them, they slowed their steps. Whatever Cress believed—either the truth that she had failed, or the untruth, which the applause might have conveyed to her, that she had succeeded—they didn't know how to greet her. Out of sorrows and disappointments, out of a flawed complexion and the death of animals and the cruelty of husbands and wives, you build yourself an edifice of escape, a funny act in which you can live for a while until your confidence returns, pretending to the outside world that everything's a big joke anyway. And then if that edifice collapses? What next? What's left? Do you give up?

They didn't know the answers—or at least any answers they thought would be as helpful as Edwin's—and they delayed their arrival as long as possible.

"John," whispered Mrs. Delahanty, clasping his arm, "why, oh why did you let me push Cress into this tragedy?"

If it *was* a tragedy, Cress didn't look it. Edwin was gone and she was in the back seat when they arrived, her horrible "Caricature in Motion" costume replaced by her usual sweater and skirt, and she was crunching Cracker Jack. Mr. Delahanty opened the back door and gazed at her.

"Hi," Cress greeted him. When he made no reply Cress said, "Well, Mother always knows best."

There was no sarcasm in her voice but Mrs. Delahanty asked, "What do you mean, Cress?"

"Making me do this act. I feel a lot better."

"Did you like the way—it went over?" Mr. Delahanty faltered, fearful of either answer.

Cress laughed. "It didn't go over. It was the lousiest act on the program. And that's saying something."

Mr. Delahanty looked for signs of dried tears, for the false heartiness of bravado. Finding neither, he said, "It wasn't the best of your acts."

"It was a flop," Cress said. "People suffered."

"You didn't seem to suffer, Cress."

"I was too busy. I was figuring."

"How to improve it?"

"That thing? I was working on what it was about."

"What *was* it about?" Mr. Delahanty asked. "I still don't know."

"Its title," Cress said, "was 'Winter.' It wasn't supposed to be funny."

"It wasn't," Mr. Delahanty agreed.

Mr. Delahanty knew that pretty soon he would ask Cress what "Winter" was about. But not right now. Now was a little interim of peace. Now he wanted to drive away from the pain of the past two hours before he invited further revelations. He slid in under the wheel, eased the car out of the parking lot, and headed toward home. In the back seat Cress was humming a tune he recognized:

"Fight on for dear old Tenant." Whatever "Winter" had been about, it had evidently been a catharsis of some kind. Though Cress had been a comedian for a month or two, she had never sung.

"Gertrude," he said, "enter me in the next Talent Contest that comes along, will you?"

"Why John, what can you do?" Mrs. Delahanty asked.

Finally he said, "I might do a little number called Spring."

PART IV

Fifteen

Spring

The interior conversations of Crescent Delahanty
started, consciously, the spring she was fifteen. In an April
twilight, the delicacy of early evening and early spring
mingling, she admitted for the first time that it was impossible to tell other people what they were determined
not to believe. But she didn't—couldn't—stop for a minute contradicting their false statements; all she could do
was stop doing this out loud. The counter-statements, the
explanations, the corrections, continued to be made,
though no longer audibly. She was full of gestures as
she listened to the untrue impressions, flurries of feeling
crossed her face; but she remained mute. That spring
she abandoned forever the belief which, in spite of set-
backs, had persisted through childhood, that to be understood one has only to tell the truth. There were some
truths which some people—particularly parents—simply
could not swallow. Particularly about their own children.
They just couldn't and it was useless to try to make them.

She was at the dining-room table memorizing geometry
theorems and their proof. The windows were open and
the scent of daphne mingled with the smell of a meat

261

loaf baking for dinner. It was about time to turn on the lights but she kept postponing it, knowing that if she stopped studying for even a minute or two, she would probably stop for good. Her mother and her mother's friend, Mrs. Agnew, were visiting in the living room. They kept their voices low, but since the two rooms were separated only by an archway, she couldn't help hearing them. When one word began to be repeated she looked up from her geometry and really listened.

"Boys!" Mrs. Agnew said, using once more the word that had caught her attention. "If any other idea ever enters Joan's head, I don't know it." Joan was Mrs. Agnew's daughter and Cress's friend. She continued, "I don't know what's happened to girls nowadays. When I was fifteen, I didn't know boys existed."

Cress awaited her mother's reply with interest, but Mrs. Delahanty had nothing to say of her own youth. Instead, she said pensively, "I don't suppose we really appreciate how lucky we are with Cress. She's never given us a minute's worry. In that regard, I mean."

"Cress is just like I was," Mrs. Agnew agreed. "Boys don't exist for her."

"I expect that's perhaps carrying it a little too far," Mrs. Delahanty admitted. "But she does have so many other interests. She debates. She plays basketball. And this spring she's mad about track meets."

Mrs. Agnew sighed so strongly the sound carried clear to the dining room. "Well, don't rub it in, Gertrude. Cress is a girl in a thousand. You can tell that just by looking at her. She'll marry late, if at all. Be a career woman of some sort. I can see her all in white, a lady M.D. Devoted to healing. Can't you? There's something so wholesome and out-of-doorsy about Cress. The way she loves plaid, for instance."

Mrs. Delahanty said, "I won't prophesy about the future, Kay, but I do admit it's a pleasure to have the boy business postponed for a while."

Cress closed her geometry book, and began, quite consciously, her interior conversation, a reply it was useless for her to make aloud. Why? Because they really *had* been different when they were fifteen? Because they had some picture of an ideal fifteen-year-old which they wanted her to fit? Because no one *ever* really sees another person? How else did they get this picture of her, the calm outdoor girl in a plaid skirt, the debater and basketball player, the yell leader; the junior M.D.

Oh Mother, oh Mrs. Agnew! Is that what you see? The girl who never thinks about boys? Why I don't ever think about anything *else*, really.

And then, because she was trying to tell the truth, she explained that "really." By "really" I don't mean all the time, but "completely." I think about geometry, of course, but not with all my mind the way I think about boys.

The first lie I ever told—that I can remember—was because of a boy. But I remember that lie exactly, and how I hated it and repented it. But I had to do it because of Tommy Fitzgerald. I was five. He was six or seven.

We had both been brought to a party and we stood by the bed where our mothers' hats were laid.

Tommy said, "That's my mother's hat. It cost $2.98." He was proud of it, he thought it was beautiful, and even I, at five, knew that a $2.98 hat was cheap and that whatever it had cost, Mrs. Fitzgerald's hat was not pretty. It was made of varnished straw and the flowers were of materials not pleasant to see or touch, faded and flimsy already, though it was new. It even smelled cheap.

"Which is your mother's hat?" Tommy asked.

I showed him. It was lavender, trimmed with lilacs deeper in color and more velvety than real lilacs, and it had a silky veil caught up with a pin with a real moonstone in it.

"How much did it cost?" Tommy asked.

It had cost ten dollars, but I heard the ashamed note in Tommy's voice. Had he praised something silly?

"Just the same," I said. That, somehow, seemed less of a lie than to say the round figures.

Tommy was relieved. He gave a snap with thumb and forefinger to the flowers of both hats—to show how unimportant hats—and mothers—and money were. "$2.98? I guess that's the regular price?" he said.

I nodded another lie. Why? Because I loved Tommy. When we moved to Tenant he gave me a ring with a blue forget-me-not for a setting. I still have it. I still remember Tommy. I still remember that lie.

When we moved to Tenant, I was nine years old and in the fifth grade. Do you remember Hubert Fairchild,

Mother? The kids called him Bert, but I never did. He's
dead now. He died during the war, but when I was nine
he was fourteen and in the eighth grade, and planning to
be a minister. Maybe he was an awful sissy—I don't know.
He came to school late, because he'd had typhoid that
summer—and his head was shaved because during the
fever most of his hair had fallen out. But I thought he
was beautiful and spiritual and I loved him.

I loved him so much that I hid my face in my desk
and cried and cried. Do you know why, Mother? Because
he had been sick and in pain and I hadn't been there to
nurse him. All that summer while I'd been carefree,
going to the beach and the mountains, *he'd* been suffering.
It broke my heart. Really I thought it did. So I cried
and cried. I told you about it. You thought I should be a
Red Cross nurse because I was so tender-hearted. I told
you as clearly as I could, but you wouldn't believe a word
I said. I cried and moped and you thought it was sickness
and suffering that made me unhappy. It wasn't. It was
Hubert.

And now? Debating? Because Calvin Dean was on the
team last year. In assembly, do you know why I sit with
my arm around the back of the seat of the girl next to
me? Because of the boys in the row behind us. To suggest
things to them. Yes, I *do*. Don't argue, don't contradict.
I *know*. I'm the one who does it. And sometimes when
I ride into town with Father at dusk, do you know what
I do? I sit close to him so people will perhaps think he's
a date. Once, a kid did. He asked me about him the next

day. "Who was the guy I saw you out with last night?"
he asked.

And track meets? Oh Mother! "Mad about track
meets." What do I care now about track meets? All that
running and jumping and sawdust pits and high and low
hurdles? Nothing, except that he is always there. But
if I tell you and Mrs. Agnew, you won't believe it; you'll
say I don't know my own mind, or what I'm talking about.
You'll say, if you do believe it, it's puppy love and too
silly to talk about. And I *won't* talk about it. But how else
can a puppy love—except like a puppy? He can't be grown
up. Or a tiger or a python.

I'm fifteen. I'm in love. I won't tell you a word about
it. But don't be dumb, Mrs. Agnew, just because I wear
a plaid skirt and am a yell leader. The way I act and the
way I feel are two different things. And don't think,
Mother, just because he's sick too that I ought to be a
Gray Lady or something.

I had heard about him before, but when I saw him I
didn't know who he was. He was always at the track
meets, dark and slender and burning-faced. He stood
very straight when he walked, but he always walked
toward something, something to lean against or sit on—
the grandstand, a marker-cart, a box of Coca-Cola. He
watched everything very intently, not just the boys running, but the movement of the glossy new leaves in the
walnut grove next to the track; or a meadow lark on a
post. He drank things in, he tipped the cup of seeing

until he had the last drop. He had to—because he's dying.

He is Mr. Cornelius. Now you know who he is. He is the father of the Cornelius boys, the track stars. The boys' names are Norman, Wayne, and Lester. They are thirteen, fifteen, and seventeen years old. Mr. Cornelius is thirty-eight. Yes, he *is* one year older than Father. His name is Mark. His wife drives one of the school buses. She is heavy, with short curly hair that sticks out from under a cap like a taxi man wears. She looks like a lady general in the Russian army. Mr. Cornelius lives in a little tent-house outside his own house so that he can have more fresh air. It is in the walnut orchard, halfway between his house and the school grounds. We can hear his radio and phonograph when we take P.E. He plays music I have never heard before.

When I go to the track meets I watch him all the time and by now he knows that I do. He smiles at me, he nods his head, he clapped once, just for me to see, when I did a particularly good back-flip, leading yells. It was silent—but I saw.

We never spoke but once. He said, "Do you know my boys?" I said "Yes." He said, "Do you like track meets?" I told him the exact truth. "Yes, but not for the same reason I used to." He knew then; I know he knew. His eyes, they're hazel, deepened and darkened. He said, "What's your name?" I told him. "Crescent Delahanty." He said, "I know your father, Crescent. I like him."

That is all we ever said to each other. But he knows,

I know he knows, I love him. I don't know whether he loves me or not but I know I am special for him. There is a special look he has for me, of tenderness, of lovingness. And not as if I were his daughter, either. It is a different look; he would put his arms around me and kiss me, I know, if I went to him, if I put my cheek to his and said "I love you."

I don't know why he would, exactly. It's not that I have any illusions about being beautiful or talented or glamorous. Is it that I understand more than anyone else how it is for him to be dying? Is it worse for him because he sees more than anyone else? Because he has more to leave behind, a thousand times as much perhaps as ordinary people? And because he was an athlete too? I've heard about it at school, how many records he broke as a boy—so he has to leave swiftness behind and grace and winning? People who have never had those, people who can only half see or half touch or who can only jog-trot, not run, and who never hear meadow larks or music, dying can't be so hard for them. Can it? And I know how hard it is for him to leave these things, because I practice all the time *being* him. I begin when I wake up in the morning by thinking, This may be my last day on earth, because whatever he suffers I want to suffer. I would do anything to save him or to make him happy.

The minute she told herself this, Cress asked herself, "Do you mean it? Would you die for him? Do you love him enough to die for him?" You must stop saying it if it isn't true. You must stop saying you love him, even, if you aren't willing to die for him, because otherwise it's just an infatuation or something. True love would give up its life a thousand times over. Fire, sword, water, torture. Nothing would matter. Think of soldiers in wartime who die for friends and how much more you feel for Mr. Cornelius than a soldier can feel for any friend.

For a long time she had known there was a thing she must do for Mr. Cornelius, a sacrifice she must offer; though for him, it would not be a sacrifice—should her offer be accepted—but the greatest joy. To give *him* life!

She stood up, and her mother called to her: "Cress, if you've finished studying, take your things to your room, will you? It's about time to set the table and Mrs. Agnew's going to stay for dinner."

Cress gathered up her books and papers and stopped in the dining room to greet Mrs. Agnew. She tried to fathom how Mrs. Agnew might have looked as a girl. It was strange how women lost, as they grew up, their own private, special look. She could tell at once what a girl was like—bright or dare-devil, prim or dull—by her looks. Girls flashed signals as to who they were, jumped, screamed, cried: they let you know. But grown-up women like Mrs. Agnew? What could you tell about her? Except that she was grown-up. She was round, she was gray, she was grown-up. She had crawled in under a smooth shell. She had heard her mother ask her father about women who looked like Mrs. Agnew, "What does her husband do?" Trying to get hold of some label which would make her different from other women just like her. Mrs. Agnew's husband was a dentist. That was the most personal thing about Mrs. Agnew.

How different Mr. Cornelius was, how much himself; how many thousand times more he was, in himself, than anything he had done. He had been an athlete, then a telephone linesman, and now he was sick and dying. But he was so much more than these things; he was like a phoenix which rose above all the realities of just existing; he, absent, was as present as Mrs. Agnew could never be. She had to look *through* Mr. Cornelius, he was so much closer and more real than Mrs. Agnew to see Mrs. Agnew at all. Mr. Cornelius who was—

Mrs. Agnew spoke, spoiling this reverie. "Now don't let us two old chatterboxes keep you from your studying, Cress. I was just telling your mother how much I admire it in you. In fact I said you were my ideal schoolgirl."

"Thank you, Mrs. Agnew," Cress said.

She went directly to the bathroom because that was the one room in the house where she could—at this time of the day, anyway—lock the door, be alone without question or interruption. She put her books on the toilet seat; then, feeling that what she was about to do needed ritualistic preparation, she thoroughly washed her hands and face, and combed her hair.

It never occurred to her that the bathroom, with its rack of toothbrushes, its laundry hamper and medicine chest, was a strange place for what she intended to do. It had been the scene, since she was a little girl, of her most intense and private feelings. She had cried more tears here than in any other room in the house. It was a room whose looks she liked—small, glistening, quiet. From the bathtub you could look out into the tops of a clump of eucalyptus trees where the buzzards roosted and could see, while your body rested fish-like in the water, the buzzards floating noiselessly in the evening air. They were not noiseless when they landed on the trees—then their wings creaked like barn doors closing on rusty hinges. Once, after a strong Santa Ana had blown the bathroom window open, she found a feather in the bathtub—as if an angel had been bathing.

When she finished combing, she put cologne on her hands and face; then she looked at herself in the mirror; not so much to *see* her face, note its size and shape, estimate its prettiness or lack of it, as to say farewell to it. This might be, if she was serious enough (and she saw nothing but seriousness in her eyes), and if God were willing, her last sight of her face. In the mirror she could see at the base of her throat the quick pulse of her heart. It jarred her with the heaviness of its thud. Her tongue felt swollen and her mouth dry. She took from the wash-basin faucet what might be her last taste of water. She let the water trickle slowly down her throat. Then she went to the window for a final look at the world.

It was that time of evening, the last minutes before complete dark, when buzzards take a bedtime flight. At this hour there seems to be an updraft from the earth so that

without any movement of their wings they hang effort-
lessly in mid-air; or soar, wings still unmoving, upward
and upward, riding on earth's breath, no longer birds but
dots on a diagram illustrating motion. The sun was already
down and a yellow scud, like foam from a broken wave,
and mud-choked, covered the western sky. The eucalyptus
trees, silhouetted against this, were filled with the interlac-
ing movement of their long brittle leaves. It was like
scissors blades crisscrossing or the soundless flutter of
pendants from a Chinese wind harp; though when a big
wind blew, the eucalyptus trees could boom like surf in
a storm.

She gazed a long time. At last she understood that she
was no longer saying farewell, only postponing. So she
said, "Farewell," out loud, went to the bathtub and knelt
with her head pressed against its rim. She hadn't planned
this position, but it did seem right for what she intended to
do, since people both prayed and were beheaded on their
knees.

She knelt there and imagined death: its nothingness, its
everlastingness. She thought of the way it might feel arriving, the terror as it approached, the possible anguish as of
bones crushed or flesh burned—only of course a million
million times worse. She tried to think, in the last seconds,
of all she was saying farewell to—her own face in the
mirror, her father and mother and outside the window, the
enormous world of which the visible yellow sky, the dark
birds and clashing leaves were the smallest, smallest part.

But then she thought of Mr. Cornelius, how the day was

probably ending for him: lying on his cot bed in his little tent-house, burning with fever, waiting for his supper tray —and waiting too for death. With this thought and at the sight of Mr. Cornelius, for she did see him behind her closed eyes, her love became exactly strong enough for what she intended to do—to offer her life for his. Not to kill herself—what good would that do—but say to God, "If it is Your holy will, please let me die and Mr. Cornelius live."

"Please let Mr. Cornelius live" did not seem to her a prayer of much strength. Who wouldn't pray that—for any sick person in the world? She certainly would gladly ask God to let every sick person in the United States get well; but she doubted that God paid much attention to such prayers. "What are *you* willing to do?" she imagined God asking the person who made such a prayer—and she didn't blame Him.

For Mr. Cornelius, she was willing to do all that she could do, she was willing to die. That was a prayer she thought God might hear, a prayer she couldn't have made, really, otherwise. Now that she was about to say the words, her throat became almost too dry to pronounce them. The blood in her forehead beat against the rim of the tub. "Dear God," she said, "I am willing to die to save Mr. Cornelius' life." She had no intention of pleading with God for Mr. Cornelius. He surely knew His own mind. But "willing" was perhaps too weak a word. She repeated her prayer, or pact—whatever it was—another way. "If it will save his life, please let me die instead of Mr. Cornelius."

She waited then. Scarcely breathing, terribly alive, ready for death. For a second she thought it was coming, that God was going to grant her prayer. Feeling was draining away, light failing, a great wave-like sound increasing; perhaps it was the sound of death arriving.

Then the sound diminished, light and feeling returned. She had not died and was not going, just then anyway, to die. However, she had placed no time limit on her offer. She hadn't said, "Now or never," to God. The pact was forever as far as she was concerned. He could change His mind any time He wanted to and take her life instead of Mr. Cornelius'. As she continued to kneel she heard her mother at the bathroom door. "Cress, Cress," she called, "we're waiting dinner for you."

She rose unsteadily and went to the window. It had grown darker but the world outside was just the same. She went again to the mirror, expecting to find in her face, anyway, some change, some evidence of renunciation or of dedication. Except for the red band across her forehead, where it had rested against the tub, her face too was unchanged. She washed in cold water and had another drink, because she still felt unsteady and a little sick at her stomach. Then she went out to the supper table.

The three of them, her father, mother, and Mrs. Agnew were already seated. Mrs. Agnew said, "Studying, home on time for meals, no make-up! Joanie is just going to hate you, Cress, if I keep holding you up to her as an example, the way I do."

"Thank you, Mrs. Agnew," Cress said.

She helped herself to the fish which might contain the bone which would be the means of her keeping her pact and said mutely, I love you, Mr. Cornelius, and think of you every minute and will gladly die for you.

Mrs. Agnew had the last word though. Pausing in the task of pulling the backbone from her fish, and shaking her head in commiseration for her own lost youth she said, "Never forget, Cress, that life will not always be so easy."

Summer

Mr. and Mrs. Delahanty, Cress, and Cress's friends, Jo Grogan and Bernadine Deevers, sat down to the Delahanty dinner table on Wednesday evening. The table was round with a white cloth that dipped at its four corners to the floor, so that in the dusk of the dining room the cloth seemed actually to be supporting the table. Mrs. Delahanty, who hadn't even expected Cress home for dinner, let alone Jo and Bernadine, felt apologetic about the food which, besides being rather uninviting, was skimpy in amount: a small salmon loaf, Harvard beets, mashed potatoes, and for dessert a cabinet pudding which did nothing to redeem the meal that had gone before. But the girls didn't seem to know or care what they put in their mouths and she decided that strawberries and fresh asparagus would have been wasted on them.

A mockingbird was singing in the orange grove outside the opened windows and the girls listened, a spoonful of cabinet pudding lifted to their opened lips—then, as the song ceased, put the spoons down without having tasted a bite. Mr. and Mrs. Delahanty had given up trying to carry on a conversation with them and treated them as so many portraits ranged round their dining room—"Girls at Dusk," or "Reveries of Youth." They talked their own talk and let the girls dream their dreams, wrap their feet around the rungs of their chairs, and listen (mouths open, eyes closed) to the bird song.

"I saw Doc Mendenhall in town today," Mr. Delahanty said.

Mrs. Delahanty said "Yes?" waiting for whatever it was that made this fact worth reporting, but Bernadine interrupted his train of thought, if he had one, by extending her long arms toward the darkening windows and singing very softly, "Oh night of love, oh beauteous night." Bernadine was barefooted (it was the spring's great fad at high school) though she was eighteen, and wore an elaborate blue voile dress which drifted about her like a sky-stained cloud. Bernadine was to be married the day after school was out and sometimes, Mrs. Delahanty felt, overplayed her role of bride-to-be.

It was already, unbelievably, the last week of school which, in Southern California, is the second week in June, a time climatically as well as scholastically neither one thing nor another, neither spring nor summer, neither truly school nor truly vacation. Class routines had been relaxed but not abandoned. Grade-wise, the feeling among the students was that the year was already water over the dam; still they couldn't be positive; some of the teachers were still going through the motions of setting down grades in their record books. Climatically the days started spring-like, damp and gray with threat even of one more unseasonal rain; at 1 P.M. exactly the day did an about-face, took on September inclinations. At that hour the overcast burned away and the tawny grasses, sun-bleached foothills, and smoldering flowers of full summer emerged. It was very confusing after getting up into a dripping cold which made sweaters and open fires necessary, to finish the day barefooted, hot-cheeked, and as naked as possible.

Cress and Jo both wore shorts and halters. Cress had shasta daisies tucked in the V of her halter and Jo Grogan, with those three flame-colored hibiscus in her short dark hair, might have been August itself on any calendar of girls. As the day darkened the white tablecloth grew silvery, the mockingbird retreated deeper into the orchard, and Mrs. Delahanty felt that the whole scene might be unreal, a mirage cast up into the present out of either the past or the future—that girls *had* sat in many a darkening room in years gone by and would so sit in the future; but that "now," the present minute, was unreal, only the past whisking by on its way to the future, or the future casting a long prophetic shadow to rearwards.

"Jo," she said briskly, "if you'll put some more custard on your pudding you might be able to eat it."

"I beg your pardon," said Jo. "Were you speaking to me?"

"Never mind," Mrs. Delahanty told her. "I was only urging you to eat."

"Oh food!" said Cress. "Food. Who cares about food?"

"I do," said Bernadine. "Howie adores puddings. Will

you copy down this recipe for me, Mrs. Delahanty? I plan to serve Howie a different pudding every single night for thirty nights. I already have twenty-two recipes."

"Tapioca, jello, and bread," said Jo, sing-songing. "If puddings be the food of love, cook on."

The mockingbird had ceased to sing. The leaves of the bougainvillaea vine which clambered over the dining-room wall rustled faintly. Mrs. Delahanty began taking the spoons from the serving dishes.

Mr. Delahanty remarked in the voice of a man who has had the words in mind for some time, "Doc Mendenhall says that Frank Cornelius had a bad hemorrhage this morning."

Mrs. Delahanty laid the spoons down, clattering. "Oh John!" she said. "I understood he was getting better."

There was a note in her voice of condemnation, as if Mr. Cornelius had not tried hard enough, as if he were a turncoat, a traitor to his generation—and hers. When old people sickened and died, men and women in their seventies and eighties, that was to be expected. But thirty-eight! That was a direct threat to her and John.

"I don't think he's taken very good care of himself," Mr. Delahanty explained. "You can't throw off t.b. just by wishing. You've got to co-operate, rest, stay put. I've seen Cornelius about town off and on all spring. Baseball, things like that. Staggering around half-alive. I saw him yesterday, sitting along the road out by his place. Today, a hemorrhage. He was asking for . . ."

Cress sprang to her feet, interrupting her father. "You mustn't say that. You have no right to say that." She pulled the daisies from the neck of her halter and passed them from hand to hand distractedly. "You don't have any idea what it's like to be dying. Do you?" she insisted.

Mr. Delahanty agreed instantly. "No, I don't, Crescent. The worst I ever had was a touch of shingles."

"Don't be funny," Cress said, her chin quivering. "Don't be funny about death. How can you understand how terrible it is for Mr. Cornelius to think he may die, no matter how much he takes care of himself? And that if he doesn't go out and see the sunshine and people and trees today he may never see them again. Never, never. And you were never a great athlete like Mr. Cornelius, so it's a thousand times worse for him than it would be for you to stay in bed. And you blame him. You blame him for not giving in. You blame him," she paused, trying to steady her voice. "I hate—I hate *people* who say cruel things like that." She looked at her father and Mr. Delahanty looked back. Then she dropped her daisies onto her plate amidst the uneaten salmon and beets and ran from the room.

Mrs. Delahanty, after the sound of the slammed door had stopped echoing, leaned over and began to gather up the daisies. The two girls excused themselves and left the room.

"What did I say?" Mr. Delahanty asked. "To cause all that?"

Mrs. Delahanty continued without speaking to shake bits of food from the flowers. "Gertrude, did what I said sound cruel and hateful to you?"

"No, John, not to me," she answered. "But then I'm not in love with Mr. Cornelius."

In her bedroom, Cress sat on the floor, her head on the window sill. When she felt an arm about her shoulders, Jo's by the weight and pressure, she said, "Go away, please go away and leave me alone." The arm remained where it was. Jo knew, and so did Bernadine. Not much, because there wasn't much to know, except that she had seen Mr. Cornelius three times to look at him and had spoken to him twice and that she loved him and would willingly die for him.

There was "not much to know" in what was called the outside world; but inside herself, in her dreams and imaginings there was nothing *but* Mr. Cornelius. She had decided out of her experience of loving Mr. Cornelius that the knowledge people had of one another, parents of children, anyway, was almost nothing. She could sit at the dinner table with her father and mother, answering their questions about school, but being in reality thousands of miles away in some hot dry land nursing Mr. Cornelius back to health; and her father and mother never noticed her absence in the least.

In her dreams she and Mr. Cornelius sometimes went away together, Mr. Cornelius saying, "Cress, without knowing it I have been searching for you all of my life. My sickness is no more than the sum of my disappointment, and without you I can never get well."

Sometimes in her dreams Mrs. Cornelius came to her and the gist of what she said was, "My life with Mr. Cornelius has been a failure. He has not many months to live. I do not want to stand between him and his happiness in the little time that is left. Go, with my blessing."

But for the most part Mrs. Cornelius and the Cornelius boys did not exist in her dreams; even the world, as she knew it in what was called "real life," was greatly altered; or, perhaps, simplified. Changed, anyway, so that it consisted of nothing but sunshine, a background of sand or water, and a grassy or sandy bank against which Mr. Cornelius reclined, getting well. And as he got well she waited on him, and talked to him. As a matter of fact, every thought in her mind had become part of an unending monologue directed toward the omnipresent mental image of Mr. Cornelius. Everything she saw immediately became words in a report to Mr. Cornelius; and if, by chance, some experience was so absorbing as to momentarily obscure his image, she made up for it by living the whole scene through once again just for him. Sometimes she imagined that Mr. Cornelius kissed her. She had to be careful about these imaginings however. She had never been kissed, family didn't count, of course, and since she supposed that when you were kissed by the man you loved, the sensations were near to swooning, swooning was what she nearly did whenever she had imaginings of this kind.

Most often she simply helped Mr. Cornelius as he reclined in the midst of the sunny simplified landscape, his thin beautiful face becoming tanned and fuller as his health improved; but not more beautiful. That was impossible. She doted on his hawk-nose and dark crest; she dismissed every other face she saw as pudgy and ill-shaped by comparison. In her dream she picked flowers for Mr. Cornelius, went to the library for him, read to him, smoothed his brow, sometimes kissed him and always, always gazed at him with enraptured eyes. But all the time she was imagining this life with Mr. Cornelius she suffered, because Mr. Cornelius was dying and there was nothing she could do about it; she suffered because she had feelings which she did not know how to express, suffered because she had put the core of her life outside its circumference.

She sat up, and Jo took her arm away. It was still light enough to see Bernadine on the floor leaning against the bed, and Jo by her side. The pitcher of white stock on her desk reflected what light there was, like a moon. The room was quiet and warm and full of misery.

"There is nothing you can do, Cress," Jo said. "You love him and he is dying. You can't do anything about either one. All you can do is to endure it."

"I can do something," Cress said.

"What?" Jo asked.

"I can go to Mr. Cornelius and tell him I love him."

"Oh no," Bernadine said, very shocked. "You can't do that."

"Why not?" Cress asked.

"You don't know whether he loves you or not."

"What does that have to do with it? I'm not going to him to ask him if he loves me. I'm going to tell him that I love him."

"Is that what you really want to do, Cress?" Jo asked.

"No—if you mean by want to, do I feel good about going. I feel awful about going. It makes me feel sick to my stomach to even think about it. It gives me the shakes."

Jo once again put an arm around Cress's shoulders. "It's a fact," she reported to Bernadine. "She's shaking like a leaf."

"Look, Cress," Bernadine said. "I'm almost married myself. It's just a matter of days. For all practical purposes I *am* married. You must think of Mr. Cornelius, Cress, and what he'd feel. I know if Howie was sick and maybe dying he wouldn't want some other woman coming to his sick bed and saying, 'I love you.' The first thing he'd do, I know, is say to me, 'Bernadine, throw this madwoman out.' And that's exactly what Mr. Cornelius is liable to say to you."

"I know it," Cress said bleakly.

"Well, then?" Bernadine asked, pride of reasoning in her voice. "Are you still going?"

Cress huddled silent, unanswering.

"It's probably not a very kind thing to do," Jo suggested in her deep, thoughtful voice. "Go to see him now when he's so sick."

"Oh I *know* that. If I just asked myself what was kind I would never do it. But what has kindness got to do with love? I'm not doing it to be kind to Mr. Cornelius. I'm doing it because I have to."

"Have to?" Jo reminded her, steadily. "You don't have to. Sit right here. Sit still. By morning everything will be different."

"By morning Mr. Cornelius may be dead."

"Well then," Bernadine said, "all your problems will be over. Mr. Cornelius will be dead and you'll be sad. But you won't have bothered him or made a fool of yourself."

"I don't care about making a fool of myself."

"You do care. You're still shaking. And think about Mrs. Cornelius. How's she going to feel about someone barging in on her sick husband, making passionate declarations of love?"

"It wouldn't be passionate. I would just say, very quietly, the minute I got there, 'I love you, Mr. Cornelius.' Then leave."

"Cress," Bernadine said, "what actually do you see yourself doing? You get there, the whole family is around the bed, and doctors and priests too, maybe. What are your plans? To say 'I beg your pardon but I've a little message for Mr. Cornelius'? Then push your way through them all to the bedside, drop on your knee, kiss his wasted hand and say, 'Mr. Cornelius, I love you.' Is that it?"

"Oh, don't heckle her, Bernadine," Jo said.

"What I see myself doing," said Cress, "is telling Mr. Cornelius something I have to tell him."

"How," asked Bernadine, "do you see yourself getting there?" Bernadine had Howie's car while he was in the army and she had driven the girls home from school. "Do you see yourself walking eight miles?"

"If I have to," Cress said.

"O.K.," Bernadine told her. "I'll drive you. And let's go right away and get it over with."

Mr. Cornelius was still living in the small one-room tent-house at the edge of the walnut grove in which his home stood. Here he was away from the noises of his family and was able to get the fresh air he needed. It was nine o'clock when Bernadine stopped the car in front of the Cornelius ranch. A dim light was burning inside the tent-house, but there was nothing to indicate the presence of the crowd of people she had prophesied. "Here we are," she said, turning off the engine.

Cress wished for any catastrophe, however great, which would prevent her from having to leave the car. She felt real hatred for Bernadine and Jo. Why, if they were convinced that she shouldn't come, hadn't they remained steadfast? What kind of friends were they, to give way to their better judgment so weakly? And what were her parents thinking about? Why had they permitted her to go riding off into the night? To tell a strange man she loved him? True, she hadn't told them where she was going nor that she loved a strange man. But what were parents for if not to understand without being told? She blamed them for her fright and unhappiness.

Still anything that *happened* would be better than continuing to live in a make-believe world in which she only dreamed that she told Mr. Cornelius she loved him. And she knew that if Bernadine were to start the car now she would jump out and run toward the tent-house and the declaration which would start her to living inside her dream. She opened the car door and stepped out into the night air which, after the warmth of the car, was damp and cold against her bare legs and arms.

"Cheerio," said Bernadine quite calmly as she was walking away from the car under the dark canopy of the big trees toward the dimly lighted room. Why was it so hard to do what she had set her heart on doing?

She stood at the screened door looking into the room as into a picture. Why did it seem like a picture? The small number of furnishings? Their neat arrangement, dresser balanced by table, chair by bed? The light falling from a bulb, shaded by blue paper, so that part of the room was in deep shadow? But most of all, was it picture-like because she had imagined the room and Mr. Cornelius for so long, that a frame had grown up about them in her mind? Now, would it be possible to break that frame? She opened the screen door, stepped into the room and became a part of the picture by that easy act.

Mr. Cornelius lay on a high narrow bed. He lay very straight, his head supported by three or four pillows and his hands folded across an ice pack which he held to his chest. His eyes were closed and his face, in spite of his illness, was warm with color. At the sight of him all of Cress's doubts left her. Oh Mr. Cornelius, she thought, I do truly love you and I have come at last to tell you.

Without opening his eyes Mr. Cornelius said, "Joyce, I think I'm going to be sick."

Joyce. Cress was surprised at the name. It seemed too gentle for the bus driver. "It's not Joyce, Mr. Cornelius," Cress said. "It's me."

Then Mr. Cornelius opened his eyes and Cress was enchanted all over again by the enormous blaze of being alive and searching and understanding which she saw there.

"It's Cress," he said, in a very low careful voice, "the track-meet girl." Then he closed his eyes. "I'm going to be sick," he said. "Hand me the basin."

The basin, Cress saw, was an enamel wash bowl on the night stand by the bed. She got it, put it on the bed beside Mr. Cornelius.

"Help me," Mr. Cornelius said and Cress helped him the way her mother had helped her when she was sick after her tonsils were out, by putting an arm around his shoulders and supporting him.

"Don't be scared," Mr. Cornelius whispered. "It's not a hemorrhage. I'm just going to lose my supper."

He did and afterwards he lay back against his pillows for a minute or two, then he reached up his hand and rang the bell which was suspended from the headboard of his bed.

"A glass of water," he told Cress, and Cress was holding it for him to rinse his mouth when Mrs. Cornelius arrived. Mrs. Cornelius paid no more attention to her than if she'd been some kind of device to help Mr. Cornelius—like the ice pack or the bell. She took the glass from Cress's hand, slipped her arm around her husband's shoulders and said, "Frank, Frank. Oh thank God, Frank, no more blood. Just your supper and that doesn't matter. I made you eat too much. This was to be expected. If you can swallow a bite or two later I'll fix you another. How do you feel now, honey?"

Cress had backed away from the bed. Mrs. Cornelius was wearing a housecoat or dressing gown of deep red, lightened by wreaths of tiny yellow and white flowers. What she looked like now was not a General in the Russian army but Robert Louis Stevenson's wife, "trusty, dusky, vivid and true with eyes of gold and bramble dew." Her bosom, which had spoiled the lines of her chauffeur's coat, was exactly right for pillowing an invalid's head, and her chestnut hair, curled corkscrew crisp, said "Never give up," as plain as any words, said "Fight on," said "Defy the universe." And all the time she was cradling Mr. Cornelius in her arms, and helping him rinse his mouth she was pressing her cheek to his hair and speaking comforting words through which there ran a mixture of laughing and joking.

"Take this to the bathroom and empty it," she said to

Cress when Mr. Cornelius had finished rinsing his mouth. She handed the basin to Cress and nodded toward a door at the back of the room. Cress, ordinarily too squeamish to pull off her own Band-Aids, marched away with it without a word.

When she returned Mr. Cornelius was once more against his pillows and Mrs. Cornelius was wiping his face with a damp cloth.

"Where'd you come from?" she asked Cress as she took the basin from her.

"From out there," Cress said, nodding toward the road. "The girls are waiting for me. In the car," she explained.

Mrs. Cornelius paused in her washing. "What did you come *for?*" she asked.

Cress welcomed the question. It was a wonderful help, like the upward spring of the diving board against her feet when she was reluctant to take off into deep water. Though she no longer had so great a need to say what she had come to say; some change had taken place in her since she had come into the room; what had been locked inside her and had been painful, because unsaid, had somehow, without a word being spoken, gotten itself partially expressed. She was not sure how. Nevertheless she had come to speak certain words. They were the answer to Mrs. Cornelius' question. They were *why* she had come.

So, louder than was necessary, and in a voice cracking with strain she said, "I came to tell Mr. Cornelius I loved him." Then she turned, resolutely, and said the words directly to Mr. Cornelius. "Mr. Cornelius, I love you."

At that Mrs. Cornelius laughed, not jeering, not angry, not unbelieving, but in the soft delighted way of a person who has received an unexpected gift, a pleasure never dreamed of but one come in the nick of time and most acceptable.

"Oh, Frankie," she said, running her hand through Mr. Cornelius' thick black hair, "look at what we've got here."

"What *we've* got," was what she'd said as if, Cress thought, I'd said I loved them both. And then, watching Mr. Cornelius reach for his wife's hand, she saw that there was nothing she could give to Mr. Cornelius without giving it also to Mrs. Cornelius. Because they were not two separated people. They were really one, the way the Bible said. It was an astounding discovery. It was almost too much for her. It held her motionless and speculating. She felt as if her mind, by an infusion of light and warmth, was being forced to expand to accommodate this new idea. And it was an idea which, contrary to all her expectations, she liked. It was exactly what she wanted. Not Mr. Cornelius alone on a stretch of desert sand and she kissing his wasted hand—in spite of her six months' dreaming. What she wanted was Mr. and Mrs. Cornelius. She was so happy for Mrs. Cornelius' presence she almost took and kissed *her* plump brown unwasted hand.

Mrs. Cornelius, however, was continuing her laughing murmur to her husband. "Frankie," she said, "oh Frankie, you old jackanapes. You old irresistible. What's all this

talk about being on your last legs? Done for? Caved in?
With school girls coming with professions of love? Pretty
school girls. Boy, we're not cashing in our checks just yet.
Not us. What's your name, dear?" she asked Cress.

Mr. Cornelius answered in his low half-whispering
voice. "She's John Delahanty's daughter, Crescent. They
call her Cress at school."

"Well," said Mrs. Cornelius. "I've heard the boys mention you. Where'd you see Frank?"

"At a track meet."

"I stared at her some," Mr. Cornelius said. "Reminded
me of you at her age. So alive."

"Was I ever like that?" Mrs. Cornelius asked her husband.

"That's what *I* thought about Mr. Cornelius," Cress
said.

"Alive?" asked Mrs. Cornelius.

"Oh yes. More than anyone there. More than the boys.
I thought his eyes fed on the sights," she said, daring the
poetry of her thoughts.

"Fed?" Mrs. Cornelius studied the word then accepted
it. "I see what you mean. Now Frank," she said, "will you
lie still and take care of yourself? Unknown school girls
loving you and wanting you to get well. You do, don't
you?" she asked Cress.

"Oh yes," Cress said. "I was willing to die for him."

Her voice evidently convinced Mrs. Cornelius. "Oh
Frank," she said, "school girls willing to die for you and
you not half trying."

"Mrs. Cornelius," Cress said, wanting, since even partial confession made her feel so much better, to tell everything, "I ought to tell you something else." She stumbled for words. "I ought to tell you what else I planned."

"I bet you planned to run away with Frank and nurse him back to health."

Cress was amazed. "Yes," she said, her face burning with guilt and foolishness, "yes I did. How did you know?"

"Oh Frank, don't it bring it all back to you? No wonder you were reminded of me. *I* was going to run away with the minister," she said turning to Cress. "Save him from his wife and family. And he *was* the most beautiful man in the world, Frank. You can't hold a candle to your father—never could."

Cress wanted to say something, but she couldn't settle on what. She had too many emotions to express. Exhilaration at being released from the isolation of her dreaming; relief to find that other girls had loved secretly too, but most of all joy to have acted, to have made for herself a single undivided world in which to live.

"Oh Mrs. Cornelius," she said, "oh Mrs. Cornelius . . ."

"Cress," asked Mrs. Cornelius, "can you play cards? Or checkers?"

"Yes," Cress said, "I can. I like to."

"And read out loud? Of course you can do that, can't you? Why don't you come read to Frank? And play cards with him? It gets so darn lonesome for him. I work.

The boys work, and besides they haven't got enough patience to sit still. And the good people come in and tell Frank how their uncles or mothers passed away with consumption and for him to be resigned. He needs somebody interested in living, not dying. Would you come?"

"Oh yes. If you want me—if he wants me. I could come every day all summer."

"O.K.," Mrs. Cornelius said, "we'll plan on it. Now you'd better run on. Frank's had a bad day. He's worn out."

Cress looked at Mr. Cornelius. His eyes were closed but he opened them at Mrs. Cornelius' words and made a good-by flicker with the lids.

"Good night," Cress said.

Mrs. Cornelius went to the door with her. "We'll count on you," she said once again and put a hand on Cress's shoulder and gave her a kind of humorous loving shake before she turned away.

Cress flew to the car propelled, it seemed, by the beat of her heart as a bird is propelled by the beat of its wings. The walnut leaves were alive and fluttering in the warm air and all about her mockingbirds were singing like nightingales. As she emerged from the grove she saw the June stars big and heavy-looking like June roses. This is the happiest hour of my life, she thought, and she yearned to do something lovely for the girls, something beautiful and memorable; but all she could think of was to ask them to go to town for milk shakes.

"I could stand some food," Bernadine said, "after all that waiting."

"He was sick," Cress explained, "and Mrs. Cornelius and I had to take care of him."

"Mrs. Cornelius? Did she come out?"

"Of course," Cress answered. "Wouldn't you, if Howie was sick?"

Bernadine had no answer to this. She started the car and after they had gone a mile or so Jo asked, "Did you tell him?"

"Of course."

"Does he love you?" Bernadine asked.

Cress felt sorry for Bernadine. "You're a fine one to be getting married," she said. "Of course he doesn't. He loves Joyce."

"Joyce? Who's Joyce?"

"Mrs. Cornelius. I remind him some of her. I adore Mrs. Cornelius. She is like Mrs. Robert Louis Stevenson and *they* are one person. Mr. and Mrs. Cornelius, I mean. They are truly married. I don't suppose you understand," she said, arrogant with new knowledge, "but what is for the one is for the other. I am going to help her take care of him this summer. Isn't that wonderful? Maybe I can really help him get well. Isn't this the most gloriously beautiful night? Oh, I think it's the most significant night of my life." The two girls were silent, but Cress was too full of her own emotions to notice.

When they went into the soda fountain, she looked at their reflection in the mirror and liked what she saw.

The three of them had always been proud of one another. Bernadine had glamour, Jo character, and Cress personality; that was the division they made of themselves. "Look at Bernadine, listen to Cress, and let Jo act," someone had said. Oh, but I've broken through that, Cress thought, I can act, too. She searched for some understanding of the part Mrs. Cornelius had played in that breakthrough. If she had said, "You wicked girl," or made her feel that loving was a terrible thing? Would she have been pushed back, fearful, into the narrowness of dreaming, and into dreaming's untruths? She didn't know. She couldn't hold her mind to such abstractions.

"What we want," she said to Lester Riggins, the boy at the fountain, "is simply the most stupendous, colossal, overpowering concoction you ever served."

"This a special night?" Lester asked.

"Super-special."

"How come?"

"Bernadine's going to be married."

"Known that for six months."

"Jo's been accepted for Stanford. With special praise."

"Old stuff."

"Then there's me."

"What about you?"

"I'm alive."

"That's different," Lester said. "Why didn't you tell me in the first place? How do you like it?"

"Being alive? Fine," said Cress. "Better than shooting stars."

"O.K., O.K.," Lester said. "This obviously merits the Riggins' special. Expense any issue?"

"No issue," Cress said.

He brought them something shaped, roughly, like the Eiffel Tower, but more dramatically colored.

"Here it is, girls. Here's to being alive!"

They sank their spoons in it and ate it down, their appetites equal to the whole of it, color, size, sweetness and multiplicity of ingredients.

PART V

Sixteen

Winter

The steam from the kettle had condensed on the cold window and was running down the glass in tear-like trickles. Outside in the orchard the man from the smudge company was refilling the pots with oil. The greasy smell from last night's burning was still in the air. Mr. Delahanty gazed out at the bleak darkening orange grove; Mrs. Delahanty watched her husband eat, nibbling up to the edges of the toast then stacking the crusts about his tea cup in a neat fence-like arrangement.

"We'll have to call Cress," Mr. Delahanty said, finally. "Your father's likely not to last out the night. She's his only grandchild. She ought to be here."

Mrs. Delahanty pressed her hands to the bones above her eyes. "Cress isn't going to like being called away from college," she said.

"We'll have to call her anyway. It's the only thing to do." Mr. Delahanty swirled the last of his tea around in his cup so as not to miss any sugar.

"Father's liable to lapse into unconsciousness any time," Mrs. Delahanty argued. "Cress'll hate coming and Father won't know whether she's here or not. Why not let her stay at Woolman?"

Neither wanted, in the midst of their sorrow for the good man whose life was ending, to enter into any discussion of Cress. What was the matter with Cress? What had happened to her since she went away to college? She, who had been open and loving? And who now lived inside a world so absolutely fitted to her own size and shape that she felt any intrusion, even that of the death of her own grandfather, to be an unmerited invasion of her privacy. Black magic could not have changed her more quickly and unpleasantly and nothing except magic, it seemed, would give them back their lost daughter.

Mr. Delahanty pushed back his cup and saucer. "Her place is here, Gertrude. I'm going to call her long distance now. She's a bright girl and it's not going to hurt her to miss a few days from classes. What's the dormitory number?"

"I know it, as well as our number," Mrs. Delahanty said. "But at the minute it's gone. It's a sign of my reluctance, I suppose. Wait a minute and I'll look it up."

Mr. Delahanty squeezed out from behind the table. "Don't bother. I can get it."

Mrs. Delahanty watched her husband, his usually square shoulders sagging with weariness, wipe a clear place on the steamy windowpane with his napkin. Some of the green twilight appeared to seep into the warm dingy little kitchen. "I can't ever remember having to smudge before in February. I expect you're right," he added as he went toward the phone. "Cress isn't going to like it."

Cress didn't like it. It was February, the rains had been late and the world was burning with a green fire; a green smoke rolled down the hills and burst shoulder-high in the cover crops that filled the spaces between the trees in the orange orchards. There had been rain earlier in the day and drops still hung from the grass blades, sickle-shaped with their weight. Cress, walking across the campus with Edwin, squatted to look into one of these crystal globes.

"Green from the grass and red from the sun," she told him. "The whole world right there in one raindrop."

"As Blake observed earlier about a grain of sand," said Edwin.

"O.K., show off," Cress told him. "You know it—but I saw it." She took his hand and he pulled her up, swinging her in a semi-circle in front of him. "Down there in the grass the world winked at me."

"Don't be precious, Cress," Edwin said.

"I will," Cress said, "just to tease you. I love to tease you, Edwin."

"Why?" Edwin asked.

"Because you love to have me," Cress said confidently, taking his hand. Being older suited Edwin. She remembered when she had liked him in spite of his looks; but now spindly had become spare, and the dark shadow of his beard—Edwin had to shave every day while other

boys were still just fuzzy—lay under his pale skin; and
the opinions, which had once been so embarrassingly unlike anyone else's, were now celebrated at Woolman as
being "Edwinian." Yes, Edwin had changed since that
day when she had knocked his tooth out trying to rescue
him from the mush pot. And had she changed? Did she
also look better to Edwin, almost slender now and the
freckles not noticeable except at the height of summer?
And with her new-found ability for light talk? They were
passing beneath the eucalyptus trees and the silver drops,
falling as the wind shook the leaves, stung her face, feeling at once both cool and burning. Meadow larks in the
fields which edged the campus sang in the quiet way they
have after the rain has stopped.

"Oh Edwin," Cress said, "no one in the world loves
the meadow lark's song the way I do!"

"It's not a competition," Edwin said, "you against the
world in an 'I-love-meadow-larks' contest. Take it easy,
kid. Love en as much as in you lieth, and let it go at that."

"No," she said. "I'm determined to overdo it. Listen,"
she exclaimed, as two birds sang together. "Not grieving,
nor amorous, nor lost. Nothing to read into it. Simply
music. Like Mozart. Complete. Finished. Oh it is rain
to listening ears." She glanced at Edwin to see how he
took this rhetoric. He took it calmly. She let go his hand
and capered amidst the fallen eucalyptus leaves.

"The gardener thinks you've got St. Vitus' dance,"
Edwin said.

Old Boat Swain, the college gardener whose name was

really Swain, was leaning on his hoe, watching her hoping and strutting. She didn't give a hoot about him or
what he thought.

"He's old," she told Edwin. "He doesn't exist." She
felt less akin to him than to a bird or toad.

There were lights already burning in the dorm windows. Cress could see Ardis and Nina still at their tables,
finishing their Ovid or looking up a final logarithm. But
between five and six most of the girls stopped trying to
remember which form of the sonnet Milton had used or
when the Congress of Vienna had met, and dressed for
dinner. They got out of their sweaters and jackets and
into their soft bright dresses. She knew just what she
was going to wear when she came downstairs at six to meet
Edwin—green silk like the merman's wife. They were
going to the Poinsettia for dinner, escaping salmon-wiggle
night in the college dining room.

"At six," she told him, "I'll fly down the stairs to
meet you like a green wave."

"See you in thirty minutes," Edwin said, leaving her
at the dorm steps.

The minute she opened the door, she began to hear the
dorm sounds and smell the dorm smells—the hiss and
rush of the showers, the thud of the iron, a voice singing,
"Dear old Woolman we love so well," the slap of bare
feet down the hall, the telephone ringing.

And the smells! Elizabeth Arden and Cashmere
Bouquet frothing in the showers; talcum powder falling

like snow; *Intoxication* and *Love Me* and *Devon Violet*; rubber-soled sneakers, too, and gym T-shirts still wet with sweat after basketball practice, and the smell of the hot iron on damp wool.

But while she was still listening and smelling, Edith shouted from the top of the stairs, "Long distance for you, Cress. Make it snappy."

Cress took the stairs three at a time, picked up the dangling receiver, pressed it to her ear.

"Tenant calling Crescent Delahanty," the operator said. It was her father: "Grandfather is dying, Cress. Catch the 7:30 home. I'll meet you at the depot."

"What's the matter—Cressie?" Edith asked.

"I have to catch the 7:30 Pacific Electric. Grandfather's dying."

"Oh poor Cress," Edith cried and pressed her arm about her.

Cress scarcely heard her. Why were they calling her home to watch Grandpa die, she thought, angrily and rebelliously. An old man, past eighty. He'd never been truly alive for her, never more than a rough, hot hand, a scraggly mustache that repelled her when he kissed her, an old fellow who gathered what he called "likely-looking" stones and kept them washed and polished, to turn over and admire. It was silly and unfair to make so much of his dying.

But before she could say a word, Edith was telling the girls. They were crowding about her. "Don't cry," they said. "We'll pack for you. Be brave, darling Cress. Re-

member your grandfather has had a long happy life. He
wouldn't want you to cry."

"Brave Cress—brave Cress," they said. "Just frozen."

She wasn't frozen. She was determined. She was not
going to go. It did not make sense. She went downstairs
to meet Edwin as she had planned, in her green silk,
ready for dinner at the Poinsettia. The girls had told him.

"Are you wearing that home?" he asked.

"I'm not going home," she said. "It's silly and useless.
I can't help Grandfather. It's just a convention. What
good can I do him, sitting there at home?"

"He might do you some good," Edwin said. "Had you
thought about that?"

"Why, Edwin!" Cress said. "Why, Edwin!" She had
the girls tamed, eating out of her hand, and here was
Edwin who loved her—he said so, anyway—cold and
disapproving. Looking at herself through Edwin's eyes,
she hesitated.

"Go on," Edwin said. "Get what you need and I'll
drive you to the station."

She packed her overnight bag and went with him; there
didn't seem—once she'd had Edwin's view of herself—
anything else to do. But once on the train her resentment
returned. The Pacific Electric was hot and smelled of
metal and dusty plush. It clicked past a rickety Mexican
settlement, through La Habra and Brea, where the pool
hall signs swung in the night wind off the ocean. An old
man in a spotted corduroy jacket, and his wife, with her

hair straggling through the holes in her broken net, sat in front of her.

Neat, thought Cress, anyone can be neat, if he wants to.

Her father, bareheaded, but in his big sheepskin jacket, met her at the depot. It was after nine, cold and raw.

"This is a sorry time, Cress," he said. He put her suitcase in the back of the car and climbed into the driver's seat without opening the door for her.

Cress got in, wrapped her coat tightly about herself. The sky was clear, the wind had died down.

"I don't see any sense in my having to come home," she said at last. "What good can I do Grandpa? If he's dying, how can I help?"

"I was afraid that was the way you might feel about it. So was your mother."

"Oh Mother," Cress burst out. "Recently she's always trying to put me . . ."

Her father cut her off. "That'll be about enough, Cress. Your place is at home and you're coming home and keeping your mouth shut, whatever you think. I don't know what's happened to you recently. If college does this to you, you'd better stay home permanently."

There was nothing more said until they turned up the palm-lined driveway that led to the house. "Here we are," Mr. Delahanty told her.

Mrs. Delahanty met them at the door, tired and haggard in her Indian design bathrobe.

"Cress," she said, "Grandfather's conscious now. I told

him you were coming and he's anxious to see you. You'd better go in right away—this might be the last time he'd know you."

Cress was standing by the fireplace holding first one foot then the other toward the fire. "Oh Mother, what am I to say?" she asked. "What can I say? Or does Grandfather just want to see me?"

Her father shook his head as if with pain. "Aren't you sorry your grandfather's dying, Cress? Haven't you any pity in your heart? Don't you understand what death means?"

"He's an old man," Cress said obstinately. "It's what we must expect when we grow old." Though she, of course, would never grow old.

"Warm your hands, Cress," her mother said. "Grandfather's throat bothers him and it eases him to have it rubbed. I'll give you the ointment and you can rub it in. You won't need to say anything."

Cress slid out of her coat and went across the hall with her mother to her grandfather's room. His thin old body was hardly visible beneath the covers; his head, with its gray skin and sunken eyes, lay upon the pillow as if bodiless. The night light frosted his white hair, but made black caverns of his closed eyes.

"Father," Mrs. Delahanty said. "Father." But the old man didn't move. There was nothing except the occasional hoarse rasp of an indrawn breath to show that he was alive.

Mrs. Delahanty pulled the cane-bottomed chair a little

closer to the bed. "Sit here," she said to Cress, "and rub
this into his throat and chest." She opened her father's
nightshirt so that an inch or two of bony grizzled chest
was bared. "He says that this rubbing relieves him, even
if he's asleep or too tired to speak. Rub it in with a slow
steady movement." She went out to the living room leaving the door a little ajar.

Cress sat down on the chair and put two squeamish
fingers into the jar of gray ointment; but she could see
far more sense to this than to any talking or being talked
to. If they had brought her home from school because she
was needed in helping to care for Grandpa, that she could
understand—but not simply to be present at his death.
What had death to do with her?

She leaned over him, rubbing, but with eyes shut,
dipping her fingers often into the gray grease. The rhythm
of the rubbing, the warmth and closeness of the room,
after the cold drive, had almost put her to sleep when
the old man startled her by lifting a shaking hand to the
bunch of yellow violets Edith had pinned to the shoulder
of her dress before she left Woolman. She opened her
eyes suddenly at his touch, but the old man said nothing,
only stroked the violets awkwardly with a trembling forefinger.

Cress unpinned the violets and put them in his hand.
"There, Grandpa," she said, "there. They're for you."

The old man's voice was a harsh and faltering whisper
and to hear what he said Cress had to lean very close.

"I used to—pick them—on Reservoir Hill. I was always sorry to—plow them up. Still—so sweet. Thanks," he said, "to bring them. To remember. You're like her. Your grandmother," he added after a pause. He closed his eyes, holding the bouquet against his face, letting the wilting blossoms spray across one cheek like a pulled-up sheet of flowering earth. He said one more word, not her name but her grandmother's.

The dikes about Cress's heart broke. "Oh Grandpa, I love you," she said. He heard her. He knew what she said, his fingers returned the pressure of her hand. "You were always so good to me. You were young and you loved flowers." Then she said what was her great discovery. "And you still do. You still love yellow violets, Grandpa, just like me."

At the sound of her uncontrolled crying, Mr. and Mrs. Delahanty came to the door. "What's the matter, Cress?"

Cress turned, lifted a hand toward them. "Why didn't you tell me?" she demanded. And when they didn't answer, she said, "Edwin knew."

Then she dropped her head on to her grandfather's outstretched hand and said something, evidently to him, which neither her father nor her mother understood.

"It's just the same."

CPSIA information can be obtained at www.ICGtesting.com
Printed in the USA
BVOW04s0934050215

386435BV00017B/267/P